100 FACTS

Celtic

First published in Great Britain in 2014
by Wymer Publishing
www.wymerpublishing.co.uk
Wymer Publishing is a trading name of Wymer (UK) Ltd

ISBN 978-1-908724-10-6

Edited by Jerry Bloom.

Typeset by Andy Francis.
Printed and bound by Lightning Source.

A catalogue record for this book is available from the British Library.

Cover design by Andy Francis.
Sketches by Becky Welton. © 2014.

Celtic

Steve Horton

FACT 1

1887

CELTIC FORMED THE YEAR BEFORE WHAT IS ON THE CREST

Although Celtic's crest contains the year 1888, which was the year the first game was played, the club had been formed on 6th November 1887 by Brother Walfrid at a meeting in St Mary's Roman Catholic Church Hall.

This was situated on what is now Forbes Street in the Calton district of the city. The football club was formed to help Irish immigrants living in poverty in the east end of Glasgow by raising money from crowds who paid to see games. Brother Walfrid had seen how successful Hibernian, founded by his friend Canon Hannan in Edinburgh, had been in achieving this.

Brother Walfrid had come to Glasgow in the 1870s from Sligo in north west Ireland and was headmaster of the Sacred Heart school. In 1893 he was sent to the East End of London where he helped poor children in Bethnal Green. He died in 1915 and is buried in Dumfries.

Although the church hall has now been demolished to make way for housing, St Mary's Church still stands and in 2008 the funeral service was held there for Tommy Burns. From the site of the hall the stands of Celtic Park can be seen, where a statue of Brother Walfrid was unveiled in front of the main entrance in 2005.

FACT 2

1888 CELTIC BEAT RANGERS IN FIRST MATCH

Celtic's first match took place on 28th May 1888 when they beat Rangers 5-2.

The match took place in front of around 2,000 fans at the first Celtic Park, which was about 100 metres north east of the present stadium. The size of the crowd was not as large as hoped due to the Glasgow International Exhibition that was also taking place that day.

The game had been advertised as being against a 'Rangers side', who left out a number of regular players, so that any defeat was excusable.

Wearing white shirts with a green collar, the scorer of the club's first ever goal was Neil McCallum but Tom Maley would go on to score a hat-trick in the match, with the other goal coming from James Kelly. After the game both sides attended a supper in St Mary's Church Hall.

The *Scottish Umpire* magazine predicted good things for Celtic, writing on 5th June, "It would appear as if the newly-formed Glasgow club, the Celtic FC, has a bright future before it. At any rate, if the committee can place the same eleven in the field as opposed the Rangers last Monday evening, or an equally strong one, the Celtic will not lack for patronage and support."

FACT 3

1889 LOSING THE CUP FINAL TWICE

In 1888-89 Celtic played competitive football for the first time and reached the Scottish Cup final, losing the first game as well as a second after the Scottish FA (SFA) ordered a replay.

Celtic's first game in the competition saw them beat Shettleston, another side from the east end of Glasgow, 5-0 with John O'Connor scoring all five goals. They then beat Cowlairs 5-0, Albion Rovers 4-1 and St Bernard's 4-1 before being drawn at home to Clyde.

Clyde beat Celtic 1-0, but Celtic successfully appealed due to the match finishing in darkness, a delay caused by Clyde having to remove illegal bars (an alternative to studs) from their boots. In a replay, Celtic romped to a 9-2 victory then beat East Stirling 2-1 in the quarter-final and Dumbarton 4-1 in the semi-final to set up a Hampden Park clash with Third Lanark on 2nd February.

By kick off time on the day of the final, wintry weather had left the pitch ankle deep in snow. With 18,000 fans at the ground the SFA were keen for the game to go ahead but both teams agreed to play it only as a friendly, which Third Lanark went on to win 3-0.

Two days later the SFA met to confirm this decision with some members claiming that the agreement for a friendly had been made between the clubs and had not been authorised by the SFA. But when the referee stated that the pitch was unplayable the members voted 10-8 to replay the game the following Saturday.

In the replayed game Celtic again lost, this time by the narrower margin of 2-1 with Third Lanark's winner coming late on. Despite the disappointment of this defeat it had still been a remarkable achievement for Celtic to reach the final in their first season in the competition.

FACT 4

1890
VOID GAME AND POINTS DEDUCTED IN LEAGUE DEBUT

In 1890-91 Celtic became founder members of the Scottish Football League, but their first two games became surrounded by controversy.

On 16th August Celtic got off to a bad start when they surprisingly lost 4-1 at home to Renton. The visitors led 3-1 at the interval and despite a strong second half fightback by Celtic they managed to remain firm in defence and then score a breakaway fourth goal.

However Renton were later expelled from the league for playing a friendly against a professional club, which was against the rules of the amateur league. As such their record was wiped out and Celtic's first league game in which the result stood was a 5-0 victory against Hearts at Tynecastle on 23rd August. In that game Johnny Madden and Willie Groves scored two goals each with the other coming from Peter Dowds.

Making his debut in goal against Hearts was James Bell, who had been signed from Dumbarton earlier that week, but he had very little to do. Celtic later learned however that league rules stated players can not play until two weeks after they had been registered. As such Celtic were deducted four points by the league - the two that had been gained against Hearts and another two which were won in a 5-2 victory against Cambuslang the following week. These were the first points deductions to occur in the Scottish Football League.

The four point deduction did not make any difference to Celtic's final position of third as the top two teams, Dumbarton and Rangers, both had an eight point advantage and would share the title.

FACT 5

1892 THE FIRST SCOTTISH CUP WIN

Celtic won the Scottish Cup for the first time in 1892, beating city rivals Queen's Park in a replayed final.

Celtic beat St Mirren, Kilmarnock Athletic, Cowlairs and Rangers to reach the final, which was played at Ibrox on 12th March. Due to crowd encroachment onto the pitch by some of the 40,000 crowd, the game was played as a friendly, Celtic winning 1-0.

At a meeting of the SFA a few days later, a request to have the replay the following Saturday was denied due to an international taking place. A date of 9th April was set and it was decided to charge a higher price of 2 shillings for admission to try and reduce the size of the crowd.

The admission was later reduced to 1 shilling and around 20,000 attended, seeing Queen's Park take a 1-0 lead at half time. However the Celts stormed back in the second half, Sandy McMahon and Johnny Campbell scoring two each and Queen's Park's Donald Sillars putting through his own goal to give Celtic a 5-1 victory.

The win meant Celtic had completed a Treble, having also won the Glasgow Cup and Glasgow Charity Cup that season and as a reward each of Celtic's players was presented with a new suit.

FACT 6

1892
CELTIC PARK OPENS WITH SPORTS DAY

In 1892 Celtic moved to Celtic Park but the first event there wasn't a football match, instead the club's annual sports day opened the new ground.

Due to the landlord increasing the annual rent from £50 to £450 at the old Celtic Park the club moved to the new site where they still play today, developing it into an oval shaped ground with vast terraced sections.

The ground opened on Saturday 13th August and despite heavy thunderstorms the vast majority of the crowd continued to brave the weather and watch the events, which included competitors from as far as Huddersfield and London entering running and cycling races.

The following week the first football match was held at the ground as Celtic beat Renton, now re-instated into the Scottish Football League, 4-3. 15,000 attended the game and saw Renton come from 3-1 down to level the scores at 3-3, only for Celtic to get the winning goal four minutes from time.

A journalist in the *Athletic News* said that the Celtic Park was the best ground in Britain alongside Everton's Goodison Park, which also opened that month. Another journalist said the new ground was like 'moving from the graveyard to paradise' hence the reason for many people going on to refer to the ground by that name.

FACT 7

1893 THE FIRST CHAMPIONSHIP SUCCESS

In their first season in the new ground Celtic won the Scottish League Championship for the first time, snatching the title from Rangers to complete a remarkable rise since their formation.

With two games remaining Celtic were second in the table but Rangers, who were a point ahead, had completed their fixtures. It meant that the Celts needed to win just one of their remaining two games against Leith Athletic and Third Lanark to win the championship.

Against Leith on 9th May 5,000 spectators saw Celtic dominate the game from the start but at half time the score was only 1-0, James Davidson scoring the goal. Leith started the second half as the better team but Celtic withstood the pressure and Johnny Madden got a second, with Davidson making it 3-0 soon afterwards.

Leith did manage a consolation but it didn't stop Celtic holding out for a win and moving above Rangers for their first championship which had come just five years after the club had played its first game. Celtic would be champions again the following year, this time confirming their title with a 3-2 win at home to Rangers.

FACT 8

1893
THE FIRST FLOODLIGHTS

The first game under floodlights at Celtic Park took place as long ago as 1893.

The match against Clyde was played on Christmas Day evening and attracted 5,000 fans. Poles were placed at various positions around the running track with sixteen lights being hung from them along the length of the field.

Although the lights allowed the players to be able to follow the action, they also got struck by high balls. The situation wasn't ideal for spectators either because it was a foggy evening.

The *Glasgow Herald* reported that neither side was at full strength but 2nd Division Clyde were not overawed by their more illustrious opponents and took the lead in the 25th minute. Celtic equalised ten minutes later and despite both sides going on the attack in the second half neither side could find a winner.

Clyde would be back at Celtic Park the following season after successfully being elected to the 1st Division, but it would be another 66 years before floodlights became a permanent feature at Celtic Park.

FACT 9

1895
CELTIC'S RECORD VICTORY

Celtic's all time record victory came on 26th October 1895 when they beat Dundee 11-0 in a game that was expected to have been a close one.

Before the match Celtic were second in the table after ten games, a point behind leaders Hibernian. Dundee were fourth, just two points behind Celtic and had won their last two games 4-0 and 5-1.

The start of the game was delayed slightly due to the stripes of both sides shirts being similar and Celtic were forced to change. But when the game began in front of a crowd of 10,000 it took Celtic fifteen minutes to score the first goal. However after this they became totally dominant and this coupled with Dundee's ineffectiveness led to a half time score of 6-0.

Dundee were without their captain William Hendrie but this was still no excuse for such a bad performance on their part. In the second half two of their players remained in the dressing room through injury and another carried on despite not being fully fit. The visitors actually managed to play better with nine men than eleven but this didn't stop Celtic scoring five more goals. By the end of the game eight different players were on the scoresheet and none had managed a hat-trick.

The win put Celtic top of the league on goal average and they went on to win the title that season. 11-0 remains a club and Scottish top flight record.

FACT 10

1900
SCOTTISH CUP WIN MARKS END OF RIVALRY

In 1900 Celtic beat Queen's Park 4-3 to win the Scottish Cup in a match that marked the end of what was the club's first big rivalry.

Queen's Park were the most successful Scottish club at the time, having won ten Scottish Cups. However they had refused to join the Scottish Football League as it was against their amateur principles.

Celtic beat Bo'ness, Port Glasgow Athletic, Kilmarnock and Rangers to reach the final which was played at Ibrox on 14th April in front of a crowd of 15,000.

Despite going a goal down, Celtic fought back to lead 3-1 at half time, Sandy McMahon playing a big part in the comeback by scoring one and setting up another for John Divers. Divers then made it 4-1 in the second half but Queen's Park staged a fightback and pulled the score back to 4-3, with the *Glasgow Herald* stating that the match may well have ended in a draw.

The win was Celtic's third Scottish Cup success, still seven short of Queen's Park's total. However their refusal to move to professionalism meant they would never enjoy success again and from then onwards Rangers became Celtic's main rivals.

FACT 11

1903 THE BIRTH OF THE HOOPS

After playing in plain white or green and white stripes for fifteen years Celtic changed to hoops for the 1903-04 season, a kit style that has remained ever since.

It is believed that the change to hoops came about after a Celtic director had seen St Anthony's, a Govan based club founded the previous year, play in them.

Even for the first two games of 1903-04 Celtic wore stripes but the hoops, which were much thinner than they would later become, were introduced for a home game with Third Lanark on 29th August 1903.

The hoops initially brought Celtic no luck though as the visitors, assisted by the wind, were 3-0 up at half time. In the second half Celtic had the advantage of the wind but could only manage to pull one goal back and the game ended 3-1.

Since 1903, Celtic have always worn green and white hoops, with the only changes to the kit being in relation to a 'v' or round neck, or a collar.

Other clubs in Europe to wear green and white hoops include Racing Santander, Sporting Lisbon and St Gallen. The Ants, as St Anthony's are known, currently play in the West Region of the Scottish Junior Football Association at McKenna Park.

FACT **12**

1904 THE FIRST EUROPEAN TOUR

Celtic first ventured outside the British Isles in 1904 when they became one of the earliest Scottish clubs to tour Europe.

Queen's Park had visited Denmark in 1898 but Celtic's trip to Bohemia (now part of the Czech Republic) and Austria was just as adventurous at the time. Manager Willie Maley was keen to test Celtic against other opposition and also spread the name of the club abroad.

A month after beating Rangers in the Scottish Cup final Celtic set off by train for Vienna, where they beat Austrian Cup winners Vienna Athletic Club 4-2 on 18th May.

Four days later they beat a Vienna Select side 6-1 before moving on to Prague, beating Deutscher FC 3-0 and Slavia Prague 4-1 to complete a 100% tour record. Very little information is available about the games as no journalists accompanied the players and newspapers reported the result only with no match report.

Ex Celtic player Johnny Madden had accompanied the tour and through contacts made became Slavia Prague's manager the following year, a position he held for 25 years. Celtic were back in Vienna and Prague in 1911 and have since toured all over the world, including as far away as Australia.

FACT 13

1905 CELTIC AND RANGERS PLAY OFF FOR TITLE

In 1904-05 Celtic won the first of six successive league titles, clinching the championship by beating Rangers in a play off.

Both teams finished level on 41 points after 26 games, but although Rangers had a better goal difference in those days it wasn't used to separate sides so a play off was arranged at Hampden Park on 5th May.

Due to fears of bias, a referee from England was brought to Glasgow to take charge of the game. Six weeks earlier the Scottish Cup final between the clubs had been abandoned in the closing stages with Rangers winning 2-0 after some fans invaded the pitch when Celtic forward Jimmy Quinn was sent off.

The match was certainly the most important Celtic v Rangers fixture to have been played at that time and arguably there hasn't been a more important one since. 30,000 turned up at Hampden and saw a goalless first half disrupted by fouls and offsides, with Celtic just about having a greater number of chances.

Just after the hour mark two goals in a minute gave Celtic the advantage. They were scored by James McMenemy and David Hamilton, the second of them with a shot from near the corner flag.

Rangers pulled a goal back in the 66th minute and it was a nervous final quarter of the game for Celtic, with Hamilton being spoken to at one stage by the referee for time wasting. They held on for the win though and this title marked the beginning of Celtic's first great era.

FACT 14

1907 THE FIRST DOUBLE

Celtic won the 'double' of Scottish League Championship and Scottish Cup for the first time in 1906-07, becoming the first club in Scotland to achieve the feat.

The first trophy to be secured was the cup, in which Celtic beat Clyde, Greenock Morton, Rangers and Hibernian to set up a final with Hearts.

Celtic dominated the first half but were unable to find the net and the score remained 0-0 at half time. Ten minutes after the restart Willie Orr scored a penalty to give the Celts the lead and after the defence resisted some Hearts pressure, Peter Somers scored twice to complete a 3-0 win.

On the day of the cup final Dundee moved one point clear at the top of the league after drawing 0-0 with Hibernian. However Celtic's run to the cup final meant they had a backlog of league fixtures and still had six games to play. They knew that just one more win would confirm them as champions because Dundee had now played all their games.

The following Wednesday at Partick Thistle's Meadowside ground Celtic won 2-0 thanks to goals from Alex Bennett and Jimmy Quinn to wrap up their third successive title. After securing the title Celtic eased up a little, winning one and drawing four of their last five games before going on a tour of Denmark.

Celtic won the double again the following season and in 1913-14. No other club acheived the feat until Rangers in 1927-28.

FACT 15

1909 NOBODY WINS THE SCOTTISH CUP FINAL

When Celtic played Rangers in the Scottish Cup final in 1909 the SFA decided to abandon the competition at the request of both clubs following two draws.

The first match was played at Hamdpen Park on 10th April and ended in a 2-2 draw, with all the goals coming in the last fifteen minutes and Celtic scoring a later equaliser.

The teams were back at Hampden a week later and 60,000 witnessed a 1-1 draw, but the rules stated that extra time was only to be played in the event of a draw after a second replay.

Most of the fans, as well as many players were not aware of this and it was only when groundstaff began taking up the corner flags that it was clear the game was over.

There were rumours that the clubs had fixed the results as draws to guarantee more revenue, but this was an absurd suggestion given Celtic still had eight league fixtures to play before the end of the month.

Many fans then invaded the pitch and the riot went on for two hours, with wooden barricades being set on fire and goalposts being ripped up. Police who tried to intervene were attacked with whatever the rioters could get their hands on and over fifty officers were injured.

Disturbances then continued on roads into the city centre and one member of the public wrote to the *Glasgow Evening Times* that rather than have police at football matches, soldiers with bayonets would be more appropriate.

Both clubs wrote to the SFA requesting that the competition be abandoned and were instead given £150 compensation for loss of revenue, while Queen's Park were paid £500 due to the damage to their stadium.

FACT 16

1909
EIGHT GAMES IN TWELVE DAYS TO WIN THE LEAGUE

Celtic made up for the abandonment of the 1909 Scottish Cup competition by winning the Scottish League Championship, making use of their games in hand to clinch the title.

Celtic were in fifth place in the 1st Division after the cup final but had enough games in hand to overhaul all of the teams above them. However they faced serious fixture congestion, having to play an incredible eight games in the remaining twelve days of the season.

The quest for the title began two days after the final, when Celtic beat Hearts 2-1 at Tynecastle. Two days later they drew 1-1 with Hamilton at Celtic Park, a result that left them third in the league and six points off the top, but with five games in hand on first place Dundee who had only one game to play.

The day after the Hamilton game they were back at Celtic Park and beat Morton 5-1, before drawing 0-0 with Airdrie, again at home, on 24th April. With Dundee having now completed their fixtures and second place Clyde being four points behind with only one game to go, Celtic knew that three wins from their last four games would guarantee the title, otherwise it would be going to Dens Park.

On 26th April Motherwell were beaten 4-0 at Celtic Park, then two days later Celtic won 5-0 at Hamdpen Park against Queen's Park. Celtic's goal average now meant that a point in their penultimate game at Easter Road against Hibernian the following evening would guarantee the title, but they lost 1-0 and it all came down to the last game, away to Hamilton. Despite obvious tiredness Celtic still had it in them to win 2-1, David Hamilton and Jimmy McMenemy scoring the goals with the home side's being a late consolation. It completed one of Celtic's most remarkable title triumphs.

FACT 17

1911
SIXTEEN CONSECUTIVE HOME CLEAN SHEETS

When Thomas Logan scored a consolation goal for Falkirk at Celtic Park on 19th August 1911 he became the first opposition player to score there in the league for ten months.

Celtic's impressive run had begun the previous November. After Rangers had won 1-0 at Celtic Park on 29th October 1910 the Celts won nine and drew three of their remaining twelve home league games without conceding a goal. However it wasn't enough to win the title as poor away form let Celtic down and they finished fifth.

On the opening day of 1911-12 Celtic beat Airdrie 3-0 to continue the clean sheet sequence, but four days later Logan scored a late goal for Falkirk in a game in which Celtic had taken a 3-0 lead.

The sequence of thirteen successive home clean sheets in the league at home has not been beaten since.

In addition to the thirteen league games, Celtic also played three Scottish Cup ties at home without conceding a goal. With Logan's goal being late in the game it meant the number of minutes played before the opposition scored stretched to over 1,500.

FACT 18

1914
CUP WIN BUT NO TROPHY FOR 74 YEARS

In 1914 Celtic won the Budapest Cup but were not presented with it until 1988.

Tours of central Europe were becoming a regular event for Celtic now and this tour to Hungary, Austria and Germany in May 1914 came after a Scottish League Championship and Scottish Cup double.

After drawing 2-2 with local side Ferencvaros, who had won five successive titles between 1909 and 1913, Celtic played a charity exhibition match against Burnley, winners of the English FA Cup. The local newspaper *Hungarian News* donated a silver trophy, the Budapest Cup, to be presented to the winners.

The game was drawn 1-1 and no extra time was played, instead a replay was agreed, which would take place in Burnley after Celtic lost the toss to decide the venue.

At Turf Moor the following September, Celtic won 2-1, with gate money from the game being sent to Budapest for distribution to charities. However the First World War broke out soon afterwards and no trophy ever made its way back to Celtic Park.

In 1988, Celtic's centenary season, Ferencvaros President Zoltan Magyar finally rectified the situation and had a special vase made which was presented to his Celtic counterpart Jack McGinn at the title winning match with Dundee in 1988.

FACT 19

1915
PLAYER AWARDED VICTORIA CROSS

In 1915 an act of extreme bravery during the First World War earned a former Celtic player the Victoria Cross, the highest military medal that can be received.

William Angus was with the club from 1912-14 but only ever played for the reserves. In 1914 he left to join junior side Wishaw Thistle and was appointed captain prior to the war breaking out in August.

On 12th June 1915 in Givenchy, France, Angus left the safety of his trench to rescue a fellow soldier who was lying injured just yards from German lines. Whilst carrying out the rescue he came under heavy fire and suffered forty wounds and lost an eye.

After spending two months in hospital he returned to Britain and was awarded the Victoria Cross by King George V on 30th August at Buckingham Palace. He was later given a standing ovation at both Celtic Park and Ibrox on 25th September 1915, when the semi-finals of the Glasgow Cup took place. The family of the soldier he saved, James Martin, sent him a telegram of thanks every year until Angus died in 1959.

Another person with Celtic connections to receive the Victoria Cross was Robert Downie, who worked on the turnstiles at the club. He was awarded the honour for capturing an enemy machine gun whilst under heavy fire at Lesboeufs in France in 1916 during the Battle of the Somme.

FACT 20

1916
TWO MATCHES IN ONE DAY

Celtic won the Scottish League Championship in 1915-16 in unusual fashion when they played twice on the same day, winning both games to clinch the title and setting a goalscoring record in the process.

The date was 15th April and it began with an afternoon fixture against Raith Rovers at Celtic Park, where 10,000 fans saw the Celts win 6-0. This took their goals tally for the season to 104, one more than Falkirk's record of 103 that had been set in 1907-08.

As Celtic were beating Raith, nearest rivals Rangers were losing 5-2 at Partick Thistle. This meant that Celtic could clinch the title if they drew at Motherwell that evening in a match that had been postponed on 25th March.

Celtic and Motherwell had the option to play the game in midweek but had decided to play twice on the Saturday instead due to the fact that the First World War was ongoing. A midweek game would mean the players and fans couldn't help the war effort by working in factories, which needed to be as productive as possible.

Several hundred fans took the train to Fir Park, where Motherwell had already played once that day, losing 3-0 to Ayr United. Only one change was made for the second game with Trooper Cassidy coming in for Joseph O'Kane. Celtic's players showed no sign of tiredness as they won 3-1 to wrap up the title, one of the goals coming from Joseph Dodds who had also scored against Raith.

The two wins meant that Celtic has secured a third title in succession and thirteenth overall.

FACT 21

1917
END OF RECORD UNBEATEN RUN

When Celtic lost 2-0 at home to Kilmarnock on 21st April 1917 in their last home game of the season, it brought to an end a remarkable run of 62 league games without defeat.

The last team to beat Celtic in the league had been Hearts, who won 2-0 when the sides met at Tynecastle on 13th November 1915. The Celts then went on the remarkable run of 49 wins and 13 draws spread over two seasons that brought the title in each of them.

Celtic had already secured the league title when Kilmarnock visited Celtic Park and some poor finishing in front of goal allowed the visitors a 2-0 win. It was second time lucky for Kilmarnock, who had been 2-1 up against the Celts with just a few minutes remaining when the two teams met at Rugby Park in February.

Celtic's defeat meant that despite the 62 game run, they had failed to match the achievement of 1897-98 when they were unbeaten all season, albeit when only eighteen games were played. In addition to the league games, they were also unbeaten in the two Glasgow Cup ties played during this period, although there was no Scottish FA Cup during the First World war.

The 62 match unbeaten run is the longest of any club in the Scottish and English leagues, although it has been bettered in Europe, with Steau Bucharest going an incredible 106 games without defeat in Romanian league games between 1986 and 1989.

FACT 22

1918 BASEBALL AT CELTIC PARK

Celtic Park's running track which was around the pitch prior to the re-development of the mid 1990s meant the stadium was often used for athletics and cycling events, while it even hosted a baseball match in 1918.

On a day when Celtic were playing Falkirk away (a match the Celts won 2-1) an international sports event was held at Celtic Park attended by 12,000 people. This was arranged to raise funds for hospitals in France where soldiers wounded in the First World War were being treated.

The event included sprint and long distance running races, a high jump and tug of war, but one of the more interesting spectacles was the baseball match, which was played between two teams of American soldiers who were based in the Clydeside area. In total the event raised £500, a considerable amount of money back then.

FACT **23**

1925 LONGEST SERVING PLAYER LEAVES

At the end of 1924-25 defender Alec McNair left Celtic after an astonishing 21 years at the club.

Signed from Stenhousemuir at the age of 20, McNair made his debut against Queen's Park in the Glasgow Cup on 10th September 1904. He went on to make 604 competitive appearances for Celtic, more than any other player.

Although a versatile player, most of his games were at right back, a position he made his own after 1908. He earned the nickname of 'The Icicle' due to his coolness as he always remained calm and composed, always judging play perfectly. He seemed to always know where the ball was coming before winning it and playing it to the midfield and forward players with ease.

One of the most remarkable achievements regarding McNair's career was that in August 1915 his wife died and he continued playing for Celtic whilst also raising five children, as well as working twelve hour shifts in a munitions factory during the First World War years.

During his time with Celtic McNair won twelve league titles, six Scottish Cups and nine Glasgow Cups. After retiring from playing in 1925 he became manager of Dundee but only remained there for two years before leaving the game and becoming a stockbroker.

FACT 24

1928
JIMMY MCGRORY SCORES EIGHT IN ONE GAME

When Celtic won 9-0 at home against Dunfermline Athletic on 14th January 1928 centre forward Jimmy McGrory scored a top flight record of eight goals in one game.

A disappointing crowd of 3,000 turned out to see if third placed Celtic could get a win that would keep them in touch with Rangers who were four points ahead of them at the top.

Dunfermline were having a miserable season and were bottom of the league without a win in eight games. The previous week they had been beaten 7-1 at home by Partick Thistle and although the nine goals scored by Celtic was not necessarily such a major surprise, the fact one player scored eight of them was.

McGrory scored all four first half goals, with his hat-trick coming after just ten minutes. Celtic could have had even more goals, but McGrory was playing so well that other forwards were trying to set him up when they were in better positions themselves.

The fifth goal was scored by John Thomson then McGrory took over again and scored four more. His eight goals was a top division record although not one for the whole league, as earlier in the season Owen McNally had scored eight for Arthurlie in a 2nd Division match against Armadale.

McGrory's goalscoring exploits weren't unnoticed in England, with Arsenal making a £10,000 bid for him at the end of the season and offering him whatever wages he wanted. However McGrory couldn't bear the thought of leaving Celtic and stayed for the rest of his playing career which lasted until 1937.

FACT 25

1931
CELTIC FINALLY GO TRANSATLANTIC

In 1931 Celtic went on a tour of North America but unlike with their earlier tours they were this time playing catch up as rivals had already gone there.

Celtic had explored the possibility of going in 1910 but felt it was unprofitable. By the time they did decide to go in 1931 Third Lanark, Rangers and Kilmarnock had already been but Celtic's tour still ended up attracting a great deal of interest.

The Celtic party sailed aboard the *Caledonia* on 13th May and were waved off by a crowd of 15,000 from Yorkhill Quay. On 22nd May they arrived in New York where they were met by several hundred ex-patriots from Scotland and Ireland, many of whom were desperate to get a glimpse of the Scottish Cup which had gone with them.

The seventeen players, management and officials stayed in America for nearly six weeks, playing thirteen matches of which nine were won, one drawn and three lost. One of the games, against New York Giants who were American League Champions, attracted a crowd of 30,000, one of the largest football crowds the USA had ever seen.

Eleven of the games were in the United States and two in Canada, with Celtic playing at famous stadiums including Fenway Park and Yankee Stadium. The tour was a great success but it would be another twenty years before any other Scottish side visited America, Celtic again being the visitors.

FACT 26

1931 JOHN THOMSON'S TRAGIC DEATH

The Old Firm match at Ibrox on 5th September 1931 had tragic consequences when Celtic's keeper John Thomson suffered a fatal injury in a collision with Rangers forward Sam English.

Thomson had become Celtic's first choice keeper towards the end of the 1926-27 season, not long after his eighteenth birthday and made 211 appearances for the club, as well as playing for Scotland four times.

Despite being only 5 feet 9 inches tall, a small height for a keeper, Thomson was thin and had amazing agility, also being able to clutch the ball well with his long fingers. He was fearless in his approach and in 1929-30 broke his jaw, two ribs and damaged his collarbone making a diving save against Airdrie.

In the fateful match with Rangers Thomson dived at the feet of Rangers forward Sam English early in the second half and his head was struck by English's knee, causing a fractured skull and ruptured artery. It was obvious to those around him that something was wrong straight away and Rangers Davie Meiklejohn quickly moved to silence some home fans mocking him behind the goal.

Thomson was taken to the Victoria Infirmary where despite an operation to try and reduce the pressure of his swelling brain he died at 9.25pm.

His funeral took place at Cardenden in Fife where he grew up. 2,000 Celtic fans went on special trains whilst many more who couldn't afford the fare walked the 55 miles to attend. Manager Willie Maley, who saw many keepers come and go, later wrote that Thomson was the greatest of them all and despite his short life he had still earned the highest honours that football had to give.

FACT 27

1936
JIMMY MCGRORY'S 50 LEAGUE GOALS

In 1935-36 Celtic secured an eighteenth league title with Jimmy McGrory hitting an astonishing fifty goals in 32 games.

The title, which was Celtic's first for ten years, was as good as secured in the last home game of the season with a 6-0 win against Ayr United. This meant second placed Rangers had to win their remaining three games by a total margin of 33 goals to overhaul them.

McGrory scored two in the first half but after sustaining an injury he was forced to play on the right wing for the second. He still managed to complete his hat-trick and he also missed a penalty.

The following Wednesday Rangers drew 1-1 at Hearts, meaning that the title was beyond doubt. McGrory's injury then kept him out of Celtic's final game at Partick Thistle, meaning he was unable to overhaul Willie MacFadyen's record of 52 goals, set whilst playing for Motherwell in 1931-32.

McGrory spent one more season with Celtic before retiring in 1937. His total goal return was an amazing 472 from 445 league and cup appearances and after eight years managing Kilmarnock he came back to Celtic Park to become manager in 1945.

FACT 28

1936 THE BAREFOOTED PLAYER

In 1936 Celtic became the first European club to sign an Indian player when Mohammed Salim joined from the Mohammedam Sporting Club that had won five Calcutta League titles in the 1930s.

Salim was then persuaded to try his luck in Britain by his cousin who managed to persuade manager Willie Maley to give him a trial.

Despite playing in bare feet Salim impressed enough to be given a game for the reserves in the Scottish Alliance against Hamilton. After impressing in a 5-1 win word soon got around and the following week an impressive crowd of 7,000 (the attendance at the last first team game had been 12,000) turned out at Celtic Park to see him play against Galston.

Celtic won 7-1 and the next day's *Glasgow Herald* reported that he played barefooted except for bandages around his ankles. It said that he 'proved skilful in ball control and crossed with accuracy' but also that 'he was not fitted to stand the rigours of our type of football'.

The *Scottish Express* was more complimentary, calling him the 'Indian Juggler' and saying that he could hypnotise the crowd and hop around defenders with the ball. The *Glasgow Observer* was also raving about him, reporting: "Every ball he touched went exactly to the place he wanted it to. Not one inch was it out. His crosses into goal were simply shrieking to be nodded into the net. I wouldn't like to have calculated the score had McGrory been playing."

However Salim soon became homesick and returned to India without playing a first team game, donating his share of the gate from a match played in his honour to local orphans.

FACT 29

1937
GAME IN FRONT OF RECORD EUROPEAN CLUB CROWD

When Celtic beat Aberdeen 2-1 to win the Scottish Cup on 24th April 1937 they did so before the largest crowd that has ever watched two club sides play each other in Europe.

There was huge interest in the match as both sides were very evenly matched. Rangers had already secured the league title but with one game to play Aberdeen were in second place, ahead of Celtic on goal average and were confident that they could secure their first major trophy.

Despite the huge interest in the game it was not made all ticket and in addition to those that made it inside, thousands were locked out. John Crum gave Celtic an eleventh minute lead but within sixty seconds Aberdeen were level thanks to a goal by Matt Armstrong. Willie Buchan got the winner with eighteen minutes remaining, a goal which infuriated the Aberdeen players who believed that Jimmy McGrory had handled the ball just beforehand, but they had stood and protested rather than play to the whistle. At the end of the game they surrounded the referee to protest as Celtic celebrated a fifteenth Scottish Cup triumph.

Two attendance figures have been given over time - 146,433 and 147,365, both of which are a record crowd between two club sides in Europe and which is unlikely to ever be broken. It came only a week after 149,415 had watched Scotland play England at Hampden, a European record for an international match. However the figure is not a world record for a club match, as in 1969 an incredible 177,656 watched Flamengo play Fluminese in Brazil.

FACT 30

1937 RECORD DEFEAT

Less than a week after winning the Scottish Cup Celtic suffered a humiliating 8-0 defeat at Motherwell in their last match of the season.

Although the game, which was played on a Friday night, had no significance manager Willie Maley named the same eleven players who had played in the cup final as rotation was unheard of then.

Motherwell were in fourth place and had no chance of overhauling Celtic, but they were the hungrier side from the start and led 4-0 after half an hour. The Celts were then dealt a further blow when keeper Joe Kennaway was forced off with a shoulder injury and cup final winning goalscorer Willie Buchan took over in goal.

Celtic fought back bravely in the second half but could not find their way past a stubborn home defence. Alex Stewart then scored twice in a three minute spell midway through the half to put Motherwell 6-0 up and complete his own hat-trick.

With left back John Morrison also having now left the field as he was injured and unable to continue Celtic were down to nine men and Stewart scored two more with twelve and seven minutes remaining to take his goal tally to six and make the final scoreline 8-0.

FACT 31

1938
CELTIC PARK'S RECORD CROWD

The huge popularity of football in the years preceding the Second World War can again be demonstrated by the fact that the record attendance at Celtic Park came the year after Celtic's record Scottish Cup final crowd.

Going into the traditional New Year's Day fixture Celtic were a point ahead of Rangers at the top of the league, but Rangers had a game in hand. The game wasn't all ticket and around 10,000 were locked outside, with the attendance since having been published as 83,000 and 92,000 (either would be a record for Celtic Park).

The *Glasgow Herald* reported that the match was delayed by six minutes to allow everybody to take up position and that twice during the first half fans encroached onto the pitch due to overcrowding, with ten requiring hospital treatment due to injuries.

After dominating the first half John Divers gave Celtic a 38th minute lead and when Malcolm MacDonald converted a penalty six minutes into the second half following a handball the result was never in doubt. Divers added a third seventeen minutes before time to give Celtic their first New Year's Day win over Rangers for ten years.

It wasn't just at Celtic Park where there was a record breaking crowd. There were more than 37,000 at Easter Road to see Hibernian v Hearts which was then a record and a 2nd Division record of 19,700 turned out at Starks Park to see Raith Rovers take on East Fife. One beneficiary of the lockout at Celtic Park was Queen's Park, whose attendance for their match against Third Lanark swelled to 25,000.

Although Celtic have had higher crowds for home games in European competition played at Hampden this crowd remains a record for Celtic Park.

FACT 32

1938 WINNING THE EMPIRE CUP

In the summer of 1938 a five month exhibition to showcase the British Empire and attract investment was held in Glasgow, with Celtic emerging triumphant in the football tournament that was part of it.

Eight teams, four each from Scotland and England, took part in the competition with all the games taking place at Ibrox due to it being near the exhibition site at Ballahouston Park.

In the quarter final on 25th May Celtic drew 0-0 with Sunderland, then beat them 3-1 in a replay the following day. In the other ties both Aberdeen and Hearts were successful over Chelsea and Brentford respectfully, but Rangers were beaten 2-0 by Everton. On 3rd June Celtic beat Hearts 1-0 to set up a final with Everton, who beat Aberdeen 3-2 in the other semi-final.

This was before the days of European competition so there was huge interest in the final as Celtic sought to prove they were the best team in Britain. 92,000 attended the final, which was a tense affair and goalless after ninety minutes but in the fifth minute of extra time Johnny Crum scored the winning goal.

The trophy, a replica of the 300 feet Tait Tower which was the centrepiece of the exhibition, was presented to Celtic by the Earl of Elgin. The trophy, along with the shirt that Crum wore in the match and the ball is on display in the Celtic Museum. The Tait Tower was demolished during the Second World War in case it was used as a beacon by German bomber pilots.

FACT 33

1940 WILLIE MALEY'S RETIREMENT

February 1940 finally saw the retirement of Willie Maley, who had managed the club for an incredible 43 years.

Maley had been just 29 when he was appointed as secretary-manager in 1897. For the first decade of the club's existence they had bought a lot of players but Maley set about a policy of developing young talent, which paid off when the club won six successive league titles between 1905 and 1910.

Another successful period followed when four titles were won between 1914 and 1917, which included the 62 game unbeaten league sequence. His third great team, which included Jimmy McGrory, tasted league success in 1936 and 1938 and won the Scottish Cup in 1937.

Maley also pioneered foreign tours and in addition to managing Celtic he did a lot of charity work and owned the Bank restaurant in Queen Street, where board meetings were held and players often attended before and after matches.

Sadly Maley's management of the club ended in disappointment. Ill health had forced him to miss much of the 1938-39 season and after the outbreak of the Second World War Scottish football was organised on regional lines.

After fourteen matches of 1939-40 Celtic were bottom of the Western Division and he was persuaded by the Board to retire, the decision was announced in the match programme for the game with Morton on 10th February.

Despite the extraordinary length of Maley's time in charge, it is not a world record. West Bromwich Albion's Fred Everiss was in the post 45 years from 1902 to 1947 and at Auxerre in France, Guy Roux was manager from 1961 to 2005, a total of 44 years.

FACT 34

1945 CUP WIN ON CORNERS

In 1945 Celtic were presented with the Victory Cup for winning a charity match to celebrate VE Day, the result of it having been decided on corners.

VE Day marked the end of the Second World War in Europe due to the surrender of Germany. 8th and 9th May were declared public holidays and the committee who organised the Glasgow Charity Cup quickly proposed to hold a match between Celtic and Rangers to raise money for charity, with a cup to be presented to the winners.

However Rangers declined to take part as they were preparing for the final of the Southern League Cup against Motherwell three days later. As such Queen's Park stepped in to play the match which was held at Hampden Park.

Johnny Paton scored the Celts goal in the game which ended in a 1-1 draw but with no time for a replay the cup was awarded to Celtic on the basis they had won one more corner during the match.

The cup that Celtic were presented with has the inscription 'Presented by the Glasgow Charity Cup Committee to Commemorate Victory in Europe 1945. Match at Hampden Park Celtic v Queen's Park Won by Celtic FC.'

FACT 35

1947 THE FIRST SENDING OFF

The first occasion when a Celtic player was sent off was on 11th January 1947 when Willie Gallacher received his marching orders against Queen's Park.

The match was a Scottish League 'A' Division fixture (the 1st Division had been re-named after the Second World War) played at Hampden Park in front of 12,000 fans. Celtic were struggling in tenth place out of sixteen teams but Queen's were in an even worse position in second bottom.

Five minutes before half time with Celtic leading 2-1 the referee, who had awarded Queen's Park a controversial penalty earlier, gave a throw-in to the home side. Gallacher, perhaps still remembering the earlier decision, reacted angrily and according to the *Glasgow Herald* "was guilty of such a serious breach of good conduct towards Harnett, the Amateurs' left half, that the referee immediately ordered him to the pavilion."

Despite being down to ten men Celtic were still dominant in the second half with Gerald McAloon outstanding and only the Queen's Park keeper preventing several more goals. The deserved third goal came from McAloon in the 74th minute at a time when Celtic had been reduced to nine men, as Patrick O'Sullivan had been forced off through injury.

FACT 36

1948 LAST DAY WIN TO AVOID RELEGATION

Celtic's struggles in the years following the departure of Willie Maley reached their low point in 1947-48 when only a win in their last match of the season prevented the club from being relegated.

The Celts spent most of the season in lower to mid-table without ever entering the relegation zone, but three straight defeats prior to their last game at Dundee left them in deep trouble.

Celtic travelled to Dens Park on 17th April knowing that if they didn't win then Airdrie and Queen of the South would both be able to overhaul them if they won their remaining games.

Jock Weir, signed for £7,000 from Blackburn Rovers in February, gave Celtic the perfect start with a goal on fourteen minutes, but Dundee equalised just before half time and took the lead on the hour mark. Weir equalised midway through the second half but the winner didn't come until two minutes from time when Weir completed his hat-trick.

The win meant that Celtic had completed their games, although a glance at the league table would make alarming reading as it would appear that both Morton and Queen of the South could overhaul them. However as they were playing each other in their final game it meant Celtic were definitely safe and they never came so close to relegation again.

FACT 37

1949
THE DEMISE OF BELFAST CELTIC

In 1949 Belfast Celtic FC, a club that had close ties with Celtic, withdrew from the Irish League.

The club had been formed in 1891 and named after Celtic, adopting the same principle of raising money for local Catholics who were in need. Further connections with Celtic were the naming of their ground Celtic Park, which was dubbed "Paradise" by fans, and also wearing a green and white hooped strip.

Belfast Celtic won four successive Irish League titles in both the 1920s and 1930s. At the outbreak of the 2nd World War they were by far the most successful club in Northern Ireland. Celtic player Charlie Tully, who made 216 league appearances for the club in the 1950s, started out at Belfast Celtic in 1944 and was one of nineteen players to play for both clubs. James Blessington and Jimmy McColl are ex-Celtic players who managed Belfast Celtic.

Belfast Celtic were never a Sectarian club, but the fact they drew most of their support from the Catholic community produced tensions at games. After a Boxing Day match at Linfield in 1948, the home fans invaded the pitch after a last minute equaliser and attacked the Celtic players, one of them suffering broken leg.

Following the incident Belfast Celtic withdrew from the Irish League saying they would return after the matters were resolved. They continued to play friendlies, including one against Celtic in 1952, while in 1949 they toured the United States beating the Scottish national side. They would never re-join the Irish League however and their last friendly was against Coleraine in 1960. There is now small museum dedicated to the club in the shopping centre that stands on the site of their old ground.

FACT 38

1951
THE FIRST BLACK PLAYER

On 18th August 1951 Gil Heron became the first black player to play for Celtic, scoring on his debut.

Heron came from Jamaica and was playing in America for Detroit Corinthians when he was spotted by a Celtic scout who was accompanying the team on a tour there. He signed on 4th August and made his debut a fortnight later against Morton in a League Cup game.

Heron scored Celtic's second goal in a 2-0 win, turning in a George Tully cross. Newspapers stated that his experience as a boxer and athlete had meant he adapted well to the physical nature of the Scottish game.

Despite the promising start, Heron never established himself at Celtic, playing just three more games, the last of which was against Partick Thistle on 1st December. At the end of the season he left for Third Lanark before playing in England for non-league Kidderminster Harriers.

Heron's son Gil Scott-Heron went on to become a famous musician and on occasions when he played in Glasgow, fans turned up wearing Celtic colours leading him to joke that he was upstaged by his father. Scott-Heron said that despite only being at the club for one season, his father had always looked out for Celtic's results.

FACT **39**

1953 WINNING THE CORONATION CUP

Just as they had in 1938 with the Empire Cup, Celtic were victorious again in an Anglo-Scottish tournament in 1953, held to celebrate the Coronation of Queen Elizabeth II.

As with the Empire Cup, there were four English and four Scottish teams and all the matches were played in Glasgow. The matches again attracted a great deal of interest as it allowed the best British sides to play competitive games against each other.

Despite having finished a disappointing eighth in the league, Celtic saved their very best form for this tournament. In the quarter final against English Champions Arsenal at Hampden Park they put in a brilliant performance to run out deserved 1-0 winners in front of 59,000 fans. The *Glasgow Herald* reported that "they had not only beaten them but taught them how to play football."

In the semi-finals Celtic faced Rangers' conquerors Manchester United, who were showing signs of developing into the great side they would become later in the decade before being so tragically decimated by the Munich Air Disaster. This match was again played at Hampden and although Celtic did not play the flowing football they had against Arsenal, they dug in and ground out a 2-1 win.

The final was against Hibernian, who had finished second in the Scottish League after winning the title in the two previous years. In front of a massive crowd of 117,000 at Hampden Neil Mochan, signed from Middlesbrough just before the tournament, gave the Celts the lead but in the second half Hibernian dominated, only for Johnny Bonnar to produce some miraculous saves. Jimmy Walsh made it 2-0 with three minutes to go to the delight of fans who could forget the disappointing season just gone.

FACT 40

1954
COMING GOOD AT THE END TO WIN DOUBLE

In 1953-54 Celtic won their first Scottish League Championship since 1938 and then added the Scottish Cup to it completing a remarkable double.

Celtic had shown in the Coronation Cup in May 1953 what they were capable of, but their league campaign started unspectacularly and a 2-1 defeat at Stirling Albion on 5th December left them in fifth place, five points behind leaders Queen of the South.

Celtic responded with three successive wins, including a 7-1 thrashing of Clyde at Shawfield and 1-0 defeat of Rangers at Celtic Park. Despite this there remained patches of inconsistency and the first time they went top of the league all season was when they won 3-1 at St Mirren on 7th April, when there were just three games to play.

The decisive game was away to Hibernian on 17th April, when an estimated 20,000 Celts supporters travelled to Edinburgh to see a 3-0 victory, Neil Mochan scoring the first goal after just ninety seconds.

The following week at Hampden Park Celtic took on Aberdeen in the final of the Scottish Cup in front of over 130,000 fans. In a close game Mochan's 51st minute shot deflected off Young into the net to give Celtic the lead, but within two minutes Aberdeen were level. However in the 65th minute Sean Fallon got the winning goal to complete what was Celtic's most memorable season of the 1950s.

FACT 41

1956 LEAGUE CUP WIN IN FIRST ALL GLASGOW FINAL

Although it took Celtic just three years to win the Scottish League Championship four years to win the Scottish Cup, they didn't win the League Cup until the eleventh time of asking.

The competition had been inaugurated in 1946-47 and the most successful side during the first ten seasons were East Fife, who won the competition three times. Back then the competition began with a group stage played before the league season started and in 1956 Celtic topped a group that included Aberdeen, East Fife and Rangers to set up a quarter final with Dunfermline Athletic.

The Pars were easily beaten 6-0 at Celtic Park, meaning a 3-0 away defeat in the second leg made no difference. In the semi-final at Hampden Park, Celtic beat Clyde 2-0 thanks to two goals from Billy McPhail against the club from whom he had joined the Celts during the summer.

Celtic met Partick Thistle, in the final at Hampden on 27th October 1956, the first time two Glasgow sides had met in the final. Despite dominating for long periods against a side that had two players carrying injuries, the Celts couldn't convert their chances.

In extra time one of Partick's injured players retired from the game but the ten men gave Celtic an almighty scare, forcing two good saves from Dick Beattie. In the replay, which took place four days later McPhail was again a two goal hero as Celtic won 3-0, all the goals coming in the first fifteen minutes of the second half.

It gave Celtic their first League Cup but with only

31,000 attending the replay it was very low key. Twelve months later they would be picking up the trophy again in much more memorable circumstances.

FACT 42

1957
JOCK STEIN LISTENS TO CELTIC THRASH RANGERS ON RADIO

When Celtic retained the League Cup in 1957-58 they did so by getting their biggest ever win over Rangers and setting a record score in a cup final.

It was the first time the two sides had met in a cup final for thirty years and Rangers were favourites going into the game, which attracted a crowd of 82,293 and was played on 19th October in unseasonably warm conditions.

Midway through the first half Charlie Tully crossed for Sammy Wilson to give Celtic the lead and then the Celts got a deserved second a minute before half time through Neil Mochan. Billy McPhail made it 3-0 on 53 minutes but Billy Simpson gave Rangers hope when he pulled one back just before the hour.

Simpson's goal only spurred Celtic on and McPhail scored twice, on 69 and 81 minutes to complete his hat-trick with Mochan getting another in between. Rangers' 7-1 humiliation was completed in the last minute when Willie Fernie scored a penalty after McPhail had been fouled in the box.

Celtic were so dominant in the game that one report claimed Rangers were lucky not to concede ten, while their defender John Valentine never played for the club again. Celtic's centre half and future manager Jock Stein was recovering from an ankle operation and listened to the match at home on the radio but he wasn't forgotten, as the club sent a car to his home to take him to the victory celebrations.

The win gave rise to the song 'Hampden In The Sun' and the margin of victory has never been matched in a cup final in either Scotland or England.

FACT **43**

1959 FLOODLIGHT SWITCH ON

The first match played under floodlights at Celtic Park was on 12th October 1959 when Celtic played a glamour friendly with English champions Wolverhampton Wanderers.

The installation of floodlights at Celtic Park was relatively late, with Dunfermline having had theirs for over three years, while two seasons earlier Celtic had played a friendly at Dumbarton to mark the 2nd Division club's inauguration of their lights.

However, when lights were finally installed at Celtic Park at a cost of £45,000 the board claimed that they were of supreme quality with the pylons that held them being the tallest of their kind in the world. They stood at 200 feet high and were made by Edinburgh company Miller & Stables.

45,000 turned out to see the game against Wolves that marked the switch on, with each individual pylon being turned on separately and the roar getting bigger each time. This was the only thing the home fans had to cheer about that night though as the visitors were too good for Celtic.

They employed a wonderfully efficient offside trap that frustrated the Celts forwards while at the other end they were clinical with goals from Peter Broadbent and Jimmy Murray giving them a 2-0 win.

FACT 44

1960
TEAM BEGIN WEARING NUMBERS

The first time Celtic players wore numbers was for a friendly against Sparta Rotterdam at the end of 1959-60, a game that was arranged as part of a *Dutch Week* in Glasgow.

Arranged by the Netherlands Chamber of Commerce, *Dutch Week* aimed to promote the country to Glaswegian people and included street performances by bands and displays of cheese and chocolates.

Celtic's match against Sparta, who had been knocked out of the European Cup by Rangers earlier in the season, attracted 29,000 to Celtic Park and marked the end of the week of celebrations.

Before kick off crowds were treated to a shower of tulips thrown by girls from Haarlem and a motorcycle display by the Rotterdam police, the highlight of which was when two of them began to argue and refused to take part.

In the game Celtic had too much class for a Sparta side that had a league game 24 hours later, running out easy 5-1 winners. Of the numbers that were worn on the shorts, the *Glasgow Herald* described them as "an admirable scheme of figures on their pants, at the front of the left leg and back of the right."

The tradition of wearing numbers on shorts, allowing the hoops to remain unspoiled, continued until 1994 when a Scottish League directive required them to be worn on shirts.

FACT 45

1963 HAMMERED ON JIMMY JOHNSTONE'S DEBUT

Celtic's greatest ever player had a debut to forget in a 6-0 defeat at Kilmarnock, but at least there was only one way things could go for eighteen year old Jimmy Johnstone after that.

With Celtic struggling in sixth place a number of younger players were given their chance in the league fixture at Rugby Park on 27th March 1963. But they were up against a side who put in their best display for some time and overpowered the Celts, storming to a 5-0 lead within an hour and eventually winning 6-0. The following day's *Glasgow Herald* reported that "none of the visitors was above average."

Johnstone though would go on to great things with the club, being converted into a right winger by new manager Jock Stein in 1965. Known as 'Jinky', he went on to play over 500 games, winning nine league titles, a European Cup, four Scottish Cups and five League Cups.

Despite standing just five feet four inches, 'Jinky' could evade any challenges that came his way and was said by his captain Billy McNeil to be able to go past any defence. He never suffered a serious injury during his time at the club.

'Jinky' died of motor neurone disease in March 2006 at the age of just 61 and such was his regard that on the day of his funeral fans of many other clubs, including Rangers, lined the route of the procession. When Celtic played Dunfermline in the League Cup final two days later, all the players wore number seven on their shorts in his honour. In 2011 a statue of 'Jinky' was unveiled in a memorial garden on the site of his former school in Uddingston.

FACT 46

1965
JOCK STEIN'S FIRST TROPHY

Former player and reserve coach Jock Stein returned to Celtic in March 1965 to become only the club's fourth ever manager and it took just two months to win his first trophy.

It was announced on 31st January that Stein, was managing Hibernian, would become Celtic manager but only when a replacement had been found for him. That meant Stein's first game in charge of Celtic was a 6-0 win away to Airdrie on 10th March.

Prior to Stein's arrival midfielder Bertie Auld, who had played under him for the reserves in the 1950s, returned to Celtic from Birmingham City for less money than he had been sold for, while the club also progressed to the semi-finals of the Scottish Cup.

In the semi-final Celtic beat Motherwell 3-0 in a replay after a 2-2 draw to set up a final with Dunfermline, who had been managed by Stein from 1960 to 1964. It was a stern test for Stein's meticulous methods of match preparation and ability to motivate his players, as they were 2-1 down at half time. He didn't panic however, telling them to keep playing the way they were and his approach was successful, the Celts coming back to win 3-2 and claim their first Scottish Cup since 1954.

Bertie Auld was influential in the match, setting up two of the goals while Stein's decision earlier in the season to switch Bobby Murdoch to right midfield from a forward position had proved a masterstroke. Defender Billy McNeil, who scored the winning goal, was revelling in the freedom of being allowed to move forward compared to having previously been told to remain in his own half at all times.

Stein later said that the glories that followed may not have happened if Celtic hadn't won this trophy.

FACT **47**

1965 THE CELTIC VIEW

August 1965 saw the first edition of the *Celtic View*, which is still in publication today and is the oldest football club magazine in the world.

The first edition, edited by Jack McGinn who was later a Chairman of the club came out on Wednesday 11th August, cost four pence and contained a picture of the team with the Scottish Cup on the front.

The front page also stated that it aimed to keep what it described as the "legions of faithful supporters" up to date with goings on at the club using what was the first magazine of its kind in Scotland.

McGinn, who had worked for newspapers, came up with the idea as he felt that Celtic were not getting sufficient coverage in the press and also believed it was a good way for the board to communicate with supporters.

Being the official publication of the club, it has never been critical with that role being left to fanzines, the most successful of which has been *Not The View*.

Nowadays the *Celtic View* is read by over 6,000 readers, much lower than the early days when circulation reached 26,000. However in the Internet age that is not unexpected and it still remains the largest selling club magazine in the United Kingdom.

FACT 48

1966
WORLD CUP WINNERS BEATEN BEFORE NEW JUNGLE ROOF

The first match to be played in front of the newly roofed Jungle was a friendly against Manchester United on 6th August 1966, with Celtic winning 4-1 against a side that contained two World Cup winning players.

There is no definitive answer as to where the name of the Jungle had come from, but one explanation is that after the Second World War former soldiers likened the swaying mass to the jungle conditions they had left behind in Burma.

During the summer of 1966 the cinder and ash terracing was concreted over and a roof added. The first game to take place in front of the new terrace was against Manchester United, whose team contained Scots Paddy Crerand and Denis Law, football genius George Best as well as Bobby Charlton and Nobby Stiles, who had been in the England side that beat West Germany 4-2 in the World Cup final a week earlier.

In front of a crowd of 60,000 Celtic over-ran United from the kick off and were 3-1 up after fifteen minutes thanks to goals from Joe McBride, Bobby Murdoch and Bobby Lennox. After an hour Celtic scored a fourth goal in comical fashion when Stiles attempted a clearance but the ball rebounded off Bill Foulkes and into the net. Such was Celtic's dominance that Law and Charlton were both subdued while Best did not have players of sufficient quality around him to make use of the brilliant touches he showed.

The *Glasgow Herald* asked the question the following Monday if the win indicated that another successful season, as Celtic were defending the Scottish League Championship.

They were not wrong.

FACT 49

1966
FIRST TWO TROPHIES OF THE QUINTUPLE

Celtic would enjoy a phenomenal season in 1966-67 winning a treble of Scottish League Championship, Scottish Cup and League Cup for the first time then becoming champions of Europe. In addition they also won the Glasgow Cup to make it a remarkable five trophies, two of which were won before the end of 1966.

On 23rd August, Celtic gave notice of their intentions when they hammered Rangers 4-0 at Ibrox in the 1st round of the Glasgow Cup in front of over 76,000 fans. Bobby Lennox hit a hat-trick with two of his goals coming from outside the area.

In the League Cup Celtic won all six of their group games scoring 25 goals, before beating Dunfermline Athletic 9-4 on aggregate in the quarter final. A 2-0 semi-final win over Airdrie set up a final against Rangers on 29th October. Unlike the Glasgow Cup tie it was a far closer game, with only Bobby Lennox's nineteenth minute goal separating the two sides.

Nine days after winning the League Cup, Celtic faced Partick Thistle in the final of the Glasgow Cup at Celtic Park. In front of a crowd of 31,000 the result was beyond doubt by half time as Celtic raced into a 4-0 lead and there was no further scoring in the second half.

Celtic's dominance over Rangers continued in the second half of the season as they clinched the league title with a 2-2 draw at Ibrox in their second to last league match. Jimmy Johnstone scored arguably his greatest ever goal in this game, a thirty yard effort with his left foot!

This completed a domestic clean sweep of trophies

as a week earlier Celtic had beaten Aberdeen in the final of the Scottish Cup, the only domestic competition in which they hadn't faced Rangers that season.

FACT **50**

1967 LISBON LIONS OVERCOME CATENACCIO

When Celtic won the European Cup in Lisbon in 1967 they did so by using local players who played good flowing football against a side renowned for a blanket defence policy.

Inter Milan were clear favourites for the final, having won the European Cup in 1964 and 1965 but they had made few friends in the process. Their victories had been achieved by playing a style of football termed *catenaccio*, which translates from Italian as padlock. Effectively they shut down the game and looked for one goal from a counter attack to win.

Stein named his side two days before the game and promised that his team, ten of whom had been born within ten miles of Celtic Park (the odd man out was Bobby Lennox, born in Saltcoats in Ayrshire), would try to win by playing free flowing attacking football.

The game initially went as pundits predicted when Sandro Mazzola converted a penalty in the seventh minute after Jim Craig had fouled Renato Cappellini. Celtic dominated from then on but could not break through the solid Inter defence, although efforts from distance by Tommy Gemmell and Bertie Auld both hit the bar.

Finally after 63 minutes the equaliser came when Gemmell was set up by Craig and hit a powerful shot that keeper Sarti couldn't hold. With six minutes remaining, Steve Chalmers got the winner from the edge of the six yard box when he turned in Bobby Murdoch's low drive.

Afterwards Liverpool manager Bill Shankly, whose side had controversially lost to Inter in the 1965 semi-final, told Stein that he was immortal while Stein himself said he was the proudest man on God's earth.

FACT **51**

1967
LOSING WORLD CHAMPIONSHIP AND £3,000

When Celtic were beaten over three games by Argentina's Racing Club in the Inter-Continental Cup, they didn't just lose the chance to become world champions, but also had a financial shock as well.

The first leg was played in front of over 100,000 at Hampden Park on 18th October. Celtic won 1-0 thanks to a Billy McNeil header, but the game was marred by Racing's dirty tricks as they constantly kicked and spat at the Celtic players when the referee wasn't looking.

It was only a taster for what would happen in Argentina, where Racing's fans joined in the bullying. Before the game even started keeper Ronnie Simpson was hit on the head by a missile, forcing John Fallon to deputise. When Celtic were awarded a first half penalty a dozen photographers went onto the pitch to try and put Tommy Gemmell off but the power of his kick was enough to beat the keeper. Racing scored twice however and with no away goals rule in place, a play-off occurred in Uruguay's capital Montevideo three days later.

Jock Stein thought long and hard before agreeing to it. Although Argentina wasn't popular in Uruguay, it was still accessible enough for 30,000 Racing fans to travel to.

A Paraguayan referee gave little protection to the Celtic players and sent off four of them after they reacted to Argentine provocation. Racing won 1-0, then Celtic were faced with another problem as their share of the gate money was paid in cash. When they returned home the banks in Glasgow and London refused to change Uruguayan pesos and they had to be sent to New York. By the time it was converted, inflation had wiped £3,000 off its value.

FACT 52

1968 RANGERS HAND CELTIC TWO TROPHIES

When Celtic won the Glasgow Cup in 1967-68 they did so with the help of Rangers who withdrew from the competition due to other commitments before slipping up in the title race.

The Glasgow Cup competition began in August when Celtic beat Partick Thistle 5-0 in the 1st round and they were then drawn against Rangers in the semi-final. Although Clyde beat Queen's Park 2-1 in the other semi-final on 4th September no date for the Celtic-Rangers game could be found, with Rangers eventually withdrawing to concentrate on their quest for league, cup and European honours.

On 17th April, the night of the Glasgow Cup final, Rangers had already been knocked out of the Scottish Cup and Inter Cities Fairs Cup (the name at the time for what is now the Europa League) but they were a point behind Celtic in the title race with a game in hand.

As Celtic stormed to an incredible 7-0 half time lead against Clyde, fans at Hampden were anxiously listening on their radios for news from Cappielow where Rangers were playing Morton. Celts fans were delighted to hear that they were trailing 3-1 and although they came back to draw 3-3 it still meant that due to a vastly superior goal average Celtic would win a third successive title if they won their last two league games.

Maybe out of compassion for Clyde's part-time players, or maybe because their minds were on the Rangers result, Celtic added just one more goal in the second half but there were still celebrations at the end as Celtic had secured the Glasgow Cup and were in control of their title destiny. Wins over Morton and Dunfermline secured the championship while Rangers were left with none of the trophies they had pulled out of the Glasgow Cup to concentrate on.

FACT 53

1968 SEVENTEEN SUCCESSIVE AWAY WINS

In 1967-68 and at the start of 1968-69 Celtic set an incredible record of seventeen straight away league victories, stretching over an eleven month period.

After losing 1-0 against Rangers at Ibrox on 16th September 1967 Celtic then drew their next match 1-1 at home to St Johnstone, meaning they had won only one of their opening three fixtures. However, starting with a 4-0 win at St Mirren on 30th September, they won 29 of their next 31 games to win the league, clinching the title in the last match of the season with a 2-1 win against Dunfermline Athletic at East End Park.

The sixteen away wins included a 6-0 win at Kilmarnock, 6-1 victory at St Johnstone and 5-0 thumping of Dundee United, who had drawn at Celtic Park earlier in the season. The away winning sequence continued with a 3-0 win at Clyde in the opening league match of 1968-69 on 7th September 1968, before finally coming to an end a fortnight later when they drew 1-1 at Dunfermline. Had Celtic been able to win that game, they would have gone a whole calendar year without dropping a point away from home.

If domestic cup games are taken into account, the away winning sequence numbers twenty as Celtic also won the three League Cup ties they played away from home during this period too. They also won a League Cup semi-final and final at neutral Hampden Park, but were unsuccessful in international competition, losing against Racing Club in both Argentina and Uruguay in the Inter Continental Cup as well as drawing against Dynamo Kiev in the USSR in the European Cup.

FACT 54

1969 RANGERS BEATEN AT LAST IN SCOTTISH CUP FINAL

After failing to win in any of the previous four Scottish Cup finals in which they had faced Rangers, Celtic finally overcame their great rivals in 1969 with an emphatic 4-0 win to complete a domestic treble.

The match was played on 26th April and although Celtic had clinched the Scottish League Championship five days beforehand to add to the League Cup they had won earlier in the month, a close contest was predicted in this final. Celtic star Jimmy Johnstone was suspended and Rangers had stated their intentions in the semi-final, where they thrashed Aberdeen 6-1.

Billy McNeil headed Celtic into the lead after just two minutes when he broke free from his marker Alex Ferguson (who later managed Aberdeen and Manchester United) to head home a corner. Later in the first half Ferguson was lucky not to be sent off after appearing to headbutt Bobby Murdoch.

Two goals in two minutes just before half time put Celtic in total control. First Bobby Lennox raced clear to score then Connelly dispossessed John Greig and rounded the keeper to tap the ball home. Stevie Chalmers completed the scoring in the 76th minute to give Jock Stein one of the most memorable of his many triumphs as boss.

The win was Celtic's first over Rangers in a Scottish Cup final since 1904, having ended up on the losing side in 1928, 1963 and 1966 and the 1909 final having been abandoned. It was also Rangers first Scottish Cup final defeat since they lost against Kilmarnock in 1929 as they had won the last fourteen in which they had taken part in.

FACT 55

1974
CELTIC IN DEVELOPMENT OF PENALTY SHOOT-OUT

After drawing 3-3 on aggregate with Benfica in the 2nd round of the European Cup in 1969-70 Celtic went through to the quarter finals after the toss of a coin, but were still sporting enough to protest to UEFA over this unsatisfactory way of settling ties.

Celtic completely dominated the first leg against a side that had twice won the European Cup earlier in the decade and been beaten finalists in 1968. The great Eusebio hardly got a kick as goals from Tommy Gemmell, Willie Wallace and Harry Hood gave the Celts a resounding victory.

The second leg was played on a rainy night in Lisbon and only 50,000 of the expected capacity crowd of 80,000 turned out. Goals from Eusebio and Graca gave Benfica a 2-0 half time lead but the Celts held on only for Diamantino to score the crucial third goal deep into injury time when he headed in a corner, although there was some confusion as the referee appeared to blow the whistle before the kick was taken.

After both teams had left the field it was announced the score was 3-0 and extra time was played, but this couldn't separate the teams. With UEFA no longer using play-offs to settle drawn ties, both captains went into the referee's room where a coin toss took place and Billy McNeil called correctly.

As the team returned to Glasgow chairman Robert Kelly stated that it had been the most unsatisfactory way to win a tie and confirmed that the club would be writing to UEFA asking them to review the way drawn ties were settled. The following season the penalty shoot-out was introduced.

FACT 56

1970
A RECORD EUROPEAN CROWD

In 1970 Celtic reached their second European Cup final, appearing before a record crowd in the competition in the semi-final.

Celtic beat Italian side Fiorentina 3-1 on aggregate to reach the semi-finals, where they were paired with English champions Leeds United. Leeds were overwhelming favourites but in the first leg at Elland Road a George Connelly goal after just forty seconds gave Celtic a 1-0 victory.

Due to the phenomenal demand the second leg, played on 15th April, was switched to Hampden Park and was attended by a crowd of 136,505, a record for European competition that is unlikely ever to be beaten. The majority of those present fell silent on fourteen minutes when Leeds captain Billy Bremner's thirty yard shot went in off the post to level the score on aggregate.

Despite being a goal down, Celtic didn't panic and were dominant in midfield with Jimmy Johnstone playing one of his best ever games for the club. Two minutes after half time the equaliser came when John Hughes headed in Bertie Auld's corner and just four minutes later Bobby Murdoch played a one-two with Jimmy Johnstone before smashing the ball past David Harvey. There was no way back for Leeds now as Celtic deservedly reached their second European Cup final, where they faced Dutch side Feyenoord in Milan.

At the San Siro stadium Celtic were favourites and Tommy Gemmell became the first British player to score in two European Cup finals when he gave them the lead on the half hour. However within two minutes Feyenoord captain Rinus Israel had equalised and four minutes from the end of extra time Ove Kindvall got the winner.

FACT 57

1971 THE OLD FIRM GAME THAT DIDN'T MATTER

There have been many memorable games against Rangers but the New Year's game played on 2nd January 1971 stood out for different reasons. The 1-1 result was irrelevant as 66 Rangers fans died after being crushed to death on a stairway leading from the terraces.

Jimmy Johnstone gave Celtic an 89th minute lead in the game, which led to many Rangers fans departing early but Colin Stein scored an injury time equaliser. It is not true that the crush occurred as fans leaving early turned around to head back inside to see what was going on, instead the likely occurrence was that somebody stumbled and this led to a catastrophic chain of events.

Jock Stein tended to the dead and injured, while Celtic physio Bob Rooney also desperately tried to give the kiss of life to as many as he could. Among the victims were five schoolmates from the town of Markinch in Fife and an eight year old boy from Canada who was attending his first football match with his grandfather. Afterwards, Stein reacted angrily to reporters who still insensitively asked questions regarding the game itself.

The next edition of the *Celtic View* referred to it as 'Black Saturday' and Stein said, "This terrible tragedy must help to curb the bigotry and bitterness of Old Firm matches. When human life is at stake this kind of hatred seems sordid and little. Fans of both sides will never forget this disaster."

On 5th January a mass was held at St Andrew's Cathedral attended by the whole Celtic squad as well as Rangers manager Willie Waddell and a number of players.

The disaster led to the *Safety of Sports Grounds Act*, ensuring that further safety measures were put in place at large venues.

FACT 58

1972
CELTIC LOSE THEIR FIRST PENALTY SHOOT-OUT

Two seasons after appealing to UEFA to decide matches in a different way rather than the unsatisfactory coin toss, Celtic went out of the competition in the first time that they took part in a penalty shoot-out.

Celtic reached the semi-finals of the European Cup by beating B1903 Copenhagen, Sliema Wanderers and Ujpest Dozsa. They were drawn against Italian champions Inter Milan, who they had beat in the 1967 final.

After a 0-0 draw in the San Siro, a further ninety minutes of football followed by extra time in front of 75,000 at Celtic Park still couldn't produce any goals, with Inter's mean defence limiting Celtic to half chances and Evan Williams in the Celts' goal hardly having a shot to save.

In the shoot-out Sandro Mazzola converted the first kick for Inter but John Deans hit his effort over the bar. Inter converted their remaining penalties in clinical fashion, Williams being able to get his hand to only one of them. Despite Jair scoring from Inter's decisive fifth kick to settle the tie, Bobby Murdoch was still made to take Celtic's fifth penalty, although by then the television cameras had stopped the coverage.

It was the second time that Inter had progressed in fortunate circumstances, as in the 2nd round they had been beaten 7-1 by Borussia Mönchengladbach only for a replay to be ordered as their keeper had been hit by a can thrown from the crowd. They had drawn this 0-0 to progress 4-2 on aggregate. Inter lost the final against Ajax, who won the second of three successive European Cups.

FACT 59

1972
EQUALLING RECORD SCOTTISH CUP FINAL SCORE

When Celtic won the Scottish Cup in 1972 they equalled a record scoreline in the final, beating Hibernian 6-1.

Celtic beat Albion Rovers, Dundee, Hearts and Kilmarnock to reach the final where they faced a Hibernian side who had knocked out Rangers in the semi-final.

In front of over 106,000 Billy McNeil gave Celtic a second minute lead but Hibs equalised through Alan Gordon. John Deans then headed Celtic into the lead on 24 minutes.

In the second half Celtic took total control, with Jimmy Johnstone giving the defenders a torrid time and Bobby Murdoch dominating the midfield. Deans scored twice to complete his hat-trick and put the game beyond doubt and make up for the disappointment of missing a penalty against Inter a few days earlier. Lisbon Lion Bertie Auld came on as a substitute for Hibs, replacing Arthur Duncan who went off with concussion.

Lou Macari scored two late goals to equal Renton's 6-1 win over Cambuslang, set way back in 1888. This was the second time Celtic had scored six against Hibernian in a cup final, having beaten them 6-2 in the League Cup final of 1968-69.

FACT 60

1973 EIGHT IN A ROW

Of all the nine in a row titles, perhaps the closest finish was in 1972-73 when Celtic needed a last day win at Hibernian to secure their eighth successive league title.

Going into the last day of the season Celtic were a point ahead of Rangers with a far superior goal difference. However they had a tough game away to third place Hibernian, while Rangers were at home to mid-table East Fife.

It was estimated that there were 40,000 Celtic supporters in the 45,000 crowd and their nerves were eased on 22 minutes when John Deans made it 1-0. Hibernian rarely looked like getting back into the game and when Kenny Dalglish scored a second on 71 minutes there was a party atmosphere for the rest of the game.

Deans got a second with ten minutes to go leading to chants of 'Eight in a row, hello, hello' from fans, which were repeated by players in the dressing room later.

Celtic's eighth successive title extended their own record of seven set the year before, which had broken the sequence of six in succession, set by Celtic from 1905 to 1910.

The following season Celtic made it nine in a row but that was a less dramatic affair, Kenny Dalglish scoring a brilliant goal from the edge of the area as they drew 1-1 at Falkirk in their third from last game to secure the title.

FACT 61

1974 CELTIC'S ONLY DRYBROUGH CUP WIN

In 1974 Celtic won their only Drybrough Cup, a pre-season competition that they took part in on six occasions.

Qualification for the eight team tournament was based on the number of goals scored in the previous season and Celtic qualified in each of the six years it too place. The Drybrough Cup was the first sponsored competition in Scotland and the rewards for participation were quite lucrative.

Celtic reached the first three finals in 1971, 1972 and 1973, losing to Aberdeen and then twice to Hibernian. In 1974 they won 4-2 at Airdrie and 2-1 at Dundee to set up a final with Rangers at Hampden Park.

The final took place in front of 57,558 fans and Jimmy Murray gave the Celts the lead on the half hour, only for Ally Scott to equalise just before half time. There were no further goals in the second half and as the competition had an experiment of no offsides the players were jaded by extra time, in which Paul Wilson put Celtic ahead only for a George McCluskey own goal to take the game to penalties.

Unlike the tension that surrounds shoot-outs today, the pre-season nature of this competition saw many of the players smiling during what was a novelty at the time. Celtic won 4-2, with Jimmy Johnstone scoring the crucial kick after Denis Connaghan had saved two of those that he faced.

Celtic didn't get the chance to defend the Drybrough Cup the following year as the competition didn't take place again until 1979, when they were beaten 3-1 by Rangers in the final. The following year was the last time it took place, with Celtic losing 1-0 to Ayr in the first round.

FACT 62

1974
TWO HAT-TRICKS VERSUS HIBERNIAN IN A WEEK

In 1974-75 Celtic beat Hibernian 6-3 to win the League Cup, with John 'Dixie' Deans scoring his second hat-trick against them in a week.

The previous Saturday Deans had hit a hat-trick as Celtic beat Hibs 5-0 at Celtic Park in a league game. At Hampden Park the crowd of 53,848, significantly lower than normal due to a Glasgow Corporation bus strike, saw Jimmy Johnstone put Celtic 1-0 up after six minutes. Deans got the second on 34 minutes but John Harper scored for Hibs to make the score 2-1 at half time.

Paul Wilson restored Celtic's two goal advantage two minutes into the second half but Harper scored again for Hibs on 61 minutes. However Deans scored twice, the second a spectacular diving header, in a three minute spell to complete his hat-trick and give Celtic a commanding 5-2 lead midway through the second half.

Steve Murray got the sixth Celtic goal in the 74th minute and with seven minutes remaining Harper completed his hat-trick with a consolation goal for Hibs. Deans's treble meant he became the first player to score hat-tricks in both the Scottish and League Cup finals and the feat hasn't been repeated since.

It also ended a League Cup jinx for Celtic who had lost their last four finals.

FACT 63

1975
SCOTTISH CUP TRIUMPH MARKS BILLY MCNEIL'S RETIREMENT

Billy McNeil, who captained Celtic to the European Cup win in 1967 retired at the end of 1974-75 as Celtic beat Airdrie in the Scottish Cup final.

After winning nine titles in a row Celtic had a disappointing league season in 1974-75, finishing in third place eleven points behind Rangers. However there was some consolation in the cups as they beat Hibernian in the League Cup final and then reached the Scottish Cup final by beating Hibernian, Clydebank, Dumbarton and Dundee.

Paul Wilson headed Celtic into the lead only for Kevin McCann to equalise for Airdrie two minutes before half time. However Celtic responded immediately and before the break Wilson headed them back into the lead. Late in the game Bobby Lennox was brought down in the box but Wilson declined the chance to take the penalty, which Pat McCluskey instead converted to seal the win.

Although Wilson had scored twice and Kenny Dalglish had been magnificent, it was captain Billy McNeil who was given the most applause at the end of the game. The 35 year old had announced beforehand that this would be his last game and was carried shoulder high by his team mates.

During his glorious Celtic career he won 23 trophies, played 486 league games and was never substituted in any of them.

FACT 64

1975 PAUL WILSON'S FOUR DIFFERENT CUP FINAL GOALS

A week after scoring twice in the Scottish Cup final against Airdrie, Paul Wilson was on target again in the Glasgow Cup final against Rangers, the fourth final in which he had scored that season.

Celtic had beaten Partick Thistle in the semi-final and with 1975 marking Glasgow's 800th birthday, the Hampden Park final with Rangers was designated a celebration of that and was eagerly awaited. Rangers had finally ended Celtic's run of league titles and Celtic triumphed in both domestic cups. 82,000 tickets were sold meaning the crowd looked set to top the previous week's Scottish Cup final crowd of 75,000.

Torrential rain and the fact that Hampden was largely uncovered limited the attendance to 70,000. With Billy McNeil having retired after the Scottish Cup final, Jock Stein handed the captaincy to Jim Brogan for what would be the veteran left backs last game for the club. In the third minute Sandy Jardine turned the ball towards his own net and Paul Wilson helped it over the line to give Celtic the lead, but Colin Stein equalised five minutes later.

Although Wilson's first goal had been gifted to him, the same could not be said of his second, for which he beat three men before shooting past Stewart Kennedy. However, Alex Macdonald scored a second equaliser to make the score 2-2 at half time.

With no goals in the second half and the competition rule not allowing for extra time and penalties the game ended as a draw and was never re-played. Wilson's goals had created a record unlikely to be matched of having scored in four cup finals in a season. He had earlier scored in the finals of the Drybrough Cup, League Cup and Scottish Cup.

FACT 65

1977 KENNY DALGLISH DEPARTS

One of Celtic's best ever players Kenny Dalglish left the club in 1977, joining European champions Liverpool for what was then a record fee between Scottish and English clubs.

Dalglish had made his debut as a seventeen year old against Hamilton in the League Cup in 1968, but did not become a regular in the side until 1971-72. By the end of 1976-77 he had scored 168 goals in 322 games, playing either as an out and out striker or as a link player between midfield and attack. When asked what his best position was, Jock Stein replied that it was best to just "let him out on the park."

By 1977 Dalglish was ready to move on and only signed a new contract to ensure he could appear in the Scottish Cup final. His subsequent refusal to go on that summer's tour to Singapore and Australia helped force the issue and Stein seemed to have seen it coming, having signed Alfie Conn from Tottenham Hotspur the previous March.

Dalglish's last appearance was in a pre-season friendly at Dunfermline Athletic on 9th August 1977 and immediately after the game he signed for Liverpool. The huge £440,000 fee was little consolation considering Celtic struggled the following season, finishing fifth in a ten team league.

Despite the circumstances surrounding his departure, Dalglish has been voted into the greatest ever Celtic team and he remains Liverpool's best ever player in the eyes of many of their fans. However his stint as manager of Celtic towards the end of 1999-2000 was not a success, nor was his second spell in charge of Liverpool that saw him sacked in May 2012.

FACT 66

1978
A FOURTEENTH SUCCESSIVE CUP FINAL

On 18th March 1978 Celtic met Rangers in the League Cup final, the fourteenth successive season they had reached the final of the competition.

The first final of the sequence was in 1964-65 when they were beaten 2-1 by Rangers and ironically the last one ended with a 2-1 defeat by the same club. Of the fourteen finals played they won six and lost eight, with five of the victories coming in successive seasons between 1965-66 and 1970-71.

Rangers were the most common opposition faced, with Celtic playing them in six of the fourteen finals. Next were Hibernian who appeared in three of them, Dundee with two while Aberdeen, Partick Thistle and St Johnstone faced the Celts in one each.

Of the finals that were won, 1965-66 was one of the most memorable as it showed that Jock Stein's players had the mental strength in big games, although the lap of honour had to be cut short when Rangers fans invaded the pitch. The 1968-69 and 1974-75 finals both saw players score hat-tricks, each time against Hibernian.

The most sensational of the eight defeats came in 1971-72 when Partick Thistle won 4-1, having been 4-0 ahead at half time to win the trophy for the first time after three final defeats in the 1950s.

Celtic's fourteen successive final appearances is a world record in any cup competition and unlikely to be broken.

FACT 67

1978 JOCK STEIN LEAVES

After a hugely disappointing 1977-78 season Jock Stein left Celtic, following thirteen years in charge that had seen him become one of the greatest managers the game has ever seen.

Stein had suffered serious injuries in a car crash in 1975 that saw him miss most of the 1975-76 season, with assistant Sean Fallon taking charge. New signings then failed to live up to expectations and with Rangers winning the treble in 1977-78 as Kenny Dalglish wasn't replaced properly it was agreed between the board and Stein that a change was required.

Lisbon Lions captain Billy McNeil, who had been managing Aberdeen for the past year, took over as manager but Stein turned down the offer of a place on the board, believing he still had something to offer the game.

On 14th August 1978 Stein had a testimonial against Liverpool, who had just retained the European Cup and the Celts lost 3-2 in front of 62,500 fans. Stein then took over as manager of the Scotland team, leading them to the 1982 World Cup, then he tragically died on 10th September 1985 at the end of a 1986 World Cup qualifying game with Wales in Cardiff.

Scotland has produced many great managers including the legendary Sir Matt Busby, Sir Alex Ferguson and Bill Shankly, but for Celtic fans Jock Stein was the greatest of them all.

FACT 68

1979
TEN MEN WIN THE LEAGUE AGAINST RANGERS

Billy McNeil's first season in charge of Celtic ended in glory as they won the Scottish League Championship, clinching the title in the last match of the season against Rangers at Celtic Park.

The match was played on 21st May, having been postponed earlier in the season. Celtic were top of the league three points ahead of Rangers, who still had two more games to play after this one. The situation for Celtic was quite simple, if they won they would be champions, but a draw or defeat would mean Rangers could overhaul them by winning their remaining games.

A bus and rail strike in the Glasgow region limited the attendance to 52,000, a startlingly low figure given what was at stake. Things looked bad for Celtic at half time as they were 1-0 down and reduced to ten men, following John Doyle's sending off for retaliation.

In the second half Celtic refused to accept defeat and tore into Rangers, Roy Aitken equalising on 66 minutes. Eight minutes later Celtic's fans went wild as George McCluskey scored from twelve yards. Within two minutes though, Rangers were level when Bobby Russell's long range effort found its way through a crowd of players.

Celtic desperately tried for a winner and with five minutes to go George McCluskey's cross was pushed out by the keeper only to bounce off Rangers defender Colin Jackson's head and into the net.

The tension was unbearable when Rangers got a corner on the stroke of full time, but Celtic cleared it and Murdo Macleod's long range effort hit the back of the net to send the crowd delirious.

Billy McNeil said after the game it was better than anything he had done as a player, but it hadn't been recorded by television cameras for posterity as the technicians were on strike as well.

FACT 69

1980
BOBBY LENNOX THE LAST LISBON LION TO RETIRE

The last playing link with the 1967 European Cup winning side ended in 1980 when Bobby Lennox retired.

Lennox had joined in 1961 at the age of eighteen and except for a loan spell with Houston Hurricane in the North American Soccer League in 1978, he did not play professionally for any other club.

Playing as a winger or forward, he scored 304 goals in all competitions, bettered only by Jimmy McGrory. As well as the European Cup win he won eleven league titles, eight Scottish Cups and five League Cups. Born in Saltcoats in Ayrshire (thirty miles from Glasgow), Lennox has jokingly been called the outsider in the European Cup winning team, as everybody else was born within ten miles of Celtic Park.

Lennox's last match was the 1980 Scottish Cup final victory against Rangers and the following November he announced his retirement from playing and joined the coaching staff, later becoming reserve team manager.

It was something of a travesty that Lennox won only ten Scottish caps, although one of those was the memorable 3-2 win over England at Wembley in 1967, their first defeat since winning the World Cup. Lennox is still regularly involved with the club at functions.

FACT 70

1982 PAUL MCSTAY'S DEBUT

One of Celtic's best ever players Paul McStay made his league debut against Aberdeen on 30th January 1982.

The seventeen year old had made his full debut a week earlier in a low key Scottish Cup tie against Queen of the South, a game most notable for Danny McGrain's first goal in three years.

However this match at Pittodrie against Alex Ferguson's Aberdeen side, who were dark horses for the title, was a different proposition altogether.

Aberdeen showed their worth in the first minute when John McMaster gave them the lead but Celtic hit back and should have equalised two minutes later when Frank McGarvey missed an open goal from inside the six yard box.

George McCluskey and Murdo Macleod both hit the bar before Celtic eventually equalised after 26 minutes, McCluskey scoring from the penalty spot after McGarvey was fouled.

Dom Sullivan gave Celtic the lead from a deflected shot in the 71st minute then six minutes later McStay, who had done very well replacing Davie Provan in midfield, capped a fine performance by weaving his way into the box and placing the ball past Jim Leighton.

The win was Celtic's third of the season and eventually proved crucial in the title race. Aberdeen went on an amazing run of sixteen wins in seventeen games but Celtic held them off to secure the title, finishing two points ahead of the Dons.

McStay went on to play over 500 times for Celtic, earning the nickname 'The Maestro' in the 1987-88 title winning season.

Despite being captain during the lean years of the early 1990s he remained at the club, reportedly rejecting a move to Inter Milan in 1992. He retired due to injury in 1997 and now lives in Australia.

FACT 71

1984
DOUBLE INVASION OF MANCHESTER

In 1984 Celtic played two games at Manchester United's Old Trafford stadium, firstly for Lou Macari's testimonial and then when they were forced to replay a European tie.

Lou Macari, who had joined United for £200,000 in 1973, was granted a testimonial at the end of 1983-84 prior to becoming player-manager of Swindon Town. An estimated 15,000 Celts supporters travelled south to see a 1-1 draw, a game in which Macari played a half for each club.

Little did Celtic fans know at the time that they would be back at Old Trafford seven months later. In the second round of the European Cup Winners Cup, Celtic overturned a 3-1 first leg defeat against Rapid Vienna, winning 3-0 at Celtic Park to progress to the quarter finals. However, UEFA ordered a replay to be held after a Rapid player claimed to have been hit by a bottle thrown by the crowd, this was despite television replays clearly showing it fall to the ground well away from where he was.

The replay had to take place 100 miles from Celtic Park but fans were determined that this would not put them at a disadvantage and an estimated 40,000 of the 51,500 crowd had travelled from Glasgow.

Celtic attacked from the start and Roy Aitken went close twice, hitting the post on seventeen minutes. Soon afterwards though, Pacult increased Rapid's overall advantage with a breakaway goal. Celtic were unable to find a way back and to make matters worse, a member of the crowd ran onto the pitch and punched the Rapid keeper, leading to Celtic being forced to play their next European home match behind closed doors. It would be several years before Celtic began to play with confidence in Europe again.

FACT 72

1985
BROTHERS IN TEAM THAT WINS CENTENARY CUP FINAL

In 1985 Celtic won the 100th Scottish Cup final, also making history by having two brothers in their team.

Before the game there was a parade of cup winning captains with Jock Stein, Billy McNeil and Kenny Dalglish all being given a huge ovation by the Celtic support, which numbered about 50,000 in a crowd of 60,346.

Things didn't look too good for Celtic when Stuart Beedie gave Dundee United, who had never won the Scottish Cup, a 54th minute lead in a game that had rarely seen Celtic look like scoring.

With Celtic needing to increase their firepower up front, manager Davie Hay took the brave decision to replace Paul McStay and Tommy Burns with Pierce O'Leary and Brian McClair and in the 76th minute Davie Provan equalised from a free kick.

In addition to the substitutions, defender Roy Aitken moved into midfield and he was an inspiration to those around him, setting up the winning goal six minutes from time when he crossed for Frank McGarvey.

At the end of the game Paul and Willie McStay collected their winners medals, making them the first brothers to appear together in a Scottish Cup winning side.

The win was Celtic's 27th Scottish Cup but Hay's first trophy as manager after taking over following Billy McNeil's departure to Manchester City in 1983.

FACT 73

1986
DUNDEE'S ALBERT KIDD THE HERO AS CELTIC WIN TITLE

One of the most dramatic finishes to a season was in 1985-86 when Celtic snatched the Scottish League Championship from the grasp of Hearts on the last day of the season.

After Hearts lost five of their first eight games nobody could have predicted what was to come that season. They then went on an unbeaten run that stretched for 27 games, hitting the top in December and staying there until the last week of the season.

In the final round of games Hearts needed just a draw at Dundee to be confirmed as champions, while even if they lost Celtic still needed to win by three goals at St Mirren to overhaul them.

The vast majority of the 17,757 fans inside Love Street were supporting the Celts and within 54 minutes they had done more than they needed to do, racing into a 5-0 lead. However they still needed a goal at Dens Park, where with half an hour remaining Albert Kidd, who had only played five games all season, went on as a substitute.

With Dundee still having an outside chance of qualifying for Europe, there was no way they would be going easy and as the game went on, Hearts got more edgy. With six minutes remaining Dundee were awarded a corner from which Kidd smashed the ball home from close range. When news of the goal reached Love Street the Celtic fans went wild and with a minute remaining Kidd added another.

At the end of the game Celtic fans and players celebrated on the pitch although there were no hoops as the team were wearing a lime green change strip.

Albert Kidd, forever a Celtic legend, was transferred to Falkirk in the summer and now lives in Australia.

FACT 74

1987 DANNY MCGRAIN LEAVES

At the end of 1986-87 Danny McGrain, one of the best defenders ever to play for Celtic, left the club.

McGrain joined in 1967 aged seventeen, a few weeks before the European Cup final. He made his debut against Dundee United in the League Cup in August 1970 but it was not until 1972-73 that he became a regular in the side.

Although mainly a right back, he was comfortable anywhere across the back four and would never shirk a tackle. He was useful going forward too, being a good passer of the ball and able to put in a decent cross. He used to leave the goalscoring to others though, managing just thirteen in 679 games.

McGrain won seven titles, five Scottish Cups and three League Cups, captained Scotland in the 1982 World Cup and has been named in Celtic's all time best eleven.

One of his greatest moments came in 1979 when he returned to the side after sixteen months out through injury to captain them to the title, clinched with the famous 4-2 win against Rangers.

McGrain's bushy beard has made him one of Celtic's most recognisable players but despite his non-compromising play on the pitch, he was a gentleman off it. McGrain was devastated when the club released him on a free transfer at the end of 1986-87, which had seen Celtic finish in second place, six points behind Rangers.

Despite leaving Celtic McGrain still had something to offer the game and played for Hamilton in 1987-88, helping them win promotion to the Premier League. He is now on the coaching staff at Celtic.

FACT **75**

1987 THE LAST GLASGOW CUP FINAL

In 1987 Celtic ended almost 100 years of tradition when a senior side appeared in the Glasgow Cup final for the last time.

In its early days the competition was keenly contested with Celtic making a stunning debut, beating Shettleston 11-2 in a 2nd round tie on 6th October 1888. They then beat Rangers 6-1 at Ibrox in the first competitive meeting between the two sides before losing 2-0 to Queen's Park in the semi-final.

Celtic won the Glasgow Cup for the first time in 1891, beating Third Lanark 4-0 in the final and retained the trophy the following year with a 7-1 hammering of Clyde. By the outbreak of the Second World War Celtic had won the competition eighteen times but from 1945 onwards its status declined, in part with the introduction of the League Cup and later due to European competition.

Between then and 1965 Celtic won the trophy five times but there was no spell of domination by any club during this period, with Partick Thistle and Clyde winning it four and three times respectively. In 1965-66 the competition was not completed but the following season Celtic won it as part of an unprecedented quintuple. Despite its declining status, the 1974-75 final attracted a crowd of 75,000 to Hampden as it was part of the city's 800th birthday celebrations.

By the 1980s it was a second string competition for the Old Firm, although for the 1985-86 final 40,000 turned out at Ibrox, interest sparked by Graeme Souness taking charge of Rangers a few days earlier. The Celts lost that game 3-2 but there was no massive interest in seeking revenge the following year, just 15,000 being at Celtic Park to see Rangers win 1-0. For 1988-89 the Glasgow Cup was re-launched as an under 17's competition.

FACT 76

1988 THE CENTENARY DOUBLE

In 1987-88 Celtic celebrated their 100th season by winning a Scottish League Championship and Scottish Cup double, the title being secured at a dangerously packed Celtic Park.

At the start of the season Rangers, who had won the league in 1986-87 and were spending big money on English players, were favourites for the title. But Billy McNeil, back as Celtic manager after a disastrous season in England where both the sides he managed - Manchester City and Aston Villa - were relegated, spent wisely and fostered a great team spirit.

Rangers were surprisingly never in the reckoning as Hearts became the early pacesetters. However at the end of November Celtic won 1-0 at Hibernian to go top. This was the eighth of a 26 match unbeaten league run that was only ended when Hearts beat Celtic 2-1 at Tynecastle on 16th April.

The Celts defeat at Hearts had only delayed the inevitable however, with just one more point being needed from the last three games to secure the title. The following Saturday Celtic Park was full to capacity with fans spilling onto the running track for the match with Dundee. The official attendance was published as 60,800 but directors later admitted over 70,000 had gained entry.

Chris Morris gave Celtic a third minute lead and Andy Walker got two in a minute in the second half to begin one of the biggest celebrations Celtic Park has ever seen with fans singing 'Happy Birthday Dear Celtic.'

Three weeks later Celtic were celebrating again, Frank McAvennie scoring two late goals to overturn a 1-0 deficit against Dundee United in the Scottish Cup final at Hampden Park.

FACT 77

1989 TRAGEDY RESULTS IN PLAYING LIVERPOOL TWICE IN APRIL

In April 1989 Celtic played English champions Liverpool twice, although the second meeting came about at short notice under tragic circumstances.

On 4th April the two sides met in the Middle East to contest the Dubai Champions Cup at the Al Wasl Stadium. This was an unofficial contest between the champions of England and Scotland that was in its third year.

After a 1-1 draw Celtic beat Liverpool 4-2 on penalties, gaining some revenge for the meeting between the two sides in December 1986 which had also finished 1-1, with the Celts losing the shoot-out 5-3.

Just eleven days later tragedy struck Liverpool at the FA Cup semi-final that was being played at Hillsborough in Sheffield. 95 of their fans were crushed to death in a tunnel and on the terracing after a gate was opened by police to ease congestion. A 96th would die in 1993 after being in a coma for four years.

On 30th April, two weeks and a day after Hillsborough, Celtic faced Liverpool in a friendly at Celtic Park, the Reds' first game since the disaster. There was a sell out crowd of 60,000 fans, which included 5,000 from Liverpool who were given tickets in various parts of the ground as no segregation was in place.

Kenny Dalglish was given a magnificent reception as he made a rare playing appearance and he scored the first goal after twenty minutes. Liverpool went on to win 4-0 but the result didn't matter on this occasion, what was important was the part Celtic played in helping the club return to normality again.

FACT 78

1989 DZIEKANOWSKI'S FOUR GOALS NOT ENOUGH

In one of the most thrilling European games ever seen at Celtic Park, Dariusz Dziekanowski hit four goals against Partizan Belgrade but Celtic still went out of the competition.

Celtic had lost 2-1 in the first leg of the first round of this European Cup Winners Cup tie, which was played in Mostar due to crowd trouble at a previous Partizan home game.

On 27th September 49,298 fans packed Celtic Park for the return and created an electric atmosphere, but they were stunned into silence on seven minutes when Vujacic put the visitors ahead. Dziekanowski, known as 'Jacki' to the fans, levelled the scores on the night and it remained 1-1 at half time, with little indication of the drama that was to unfold in the second half.

A minute after the restart Dziekanowski put Celtic 2-1 up on the night to make it 3-3 on aggregate. There then followed an incredible fifteen minute period in which Partizan went 4-3 up, Dziekanowski made it 4-4, Partizan scored again and then Andy Walker made it 5-5. This meant with 25 minutes remaining, Celtic were 4-3 up on the night but behind due to away goals and still needed another to go through.

With nine minutes remaining Dziekanowski scored his fourth goal of the game from a Mike Galloway cross to put Celtic ahead for the first time in the tie. However there was heartbreak with little more than a minute left when Scepovic headed a crucial fourth for Partizan to send them through on away goals.

There may have been disappointment at how the game had turned out, but those that were there knew that they had witnessed something special that would be talked about for years to come.

FACT **79**

1991 BEATING EIGHT MEN RANGERS IN CUP

In the Scottish Cup quarter final on 17th March 1991 Celtic beat Rangers 2-0 in a game that saw four men sent off, including three from the opposition.

Celtic were struggling in fourth place in the league as Rangers looked set to secure a third straight title. However despite their league dominance at that time they still couldn't manage success in the Scottish Cup and hadn't won the trophy since 1991.

In a match that was live on television, a rarity at the time, Celtic were 2-0 up at half time thanks to a goal by Gerry Creaney and a forty yard free kick from Darius Wdowcyzk that took a deflection off Terry Hurlock. At the break there were still 22 players on the pitch but that would change in the second half.

It was no surprise that Rangers threw everybody forward in the second half and they were given a boost on 53 minutes when Celtic were reduced to ten men. After being booked for giving away a foul, Peter Grant was then sent off for breaking from the wall before the free kick was taken to charge it down.

Rangers increased the pressure and Celtic were up against it, but just nine minutes later Hurlock was sent off for elbowing Tommy Coyne, cutting short the Rangers revival. As they tie slipped away from them Mark Walters saw red with eleven minutes remaining for elbowing Coyne after failing to win the ball cleanly. Just three minutes later Mark Hateley, already on a yellow card, received a second booking for a reckless lunge on Anton Rogan reducing Rangers to eight men.

The match became known as the St Patrick's Day massacre but Celtic were unable to continue the momentum, losing the semi-final 4-2 to Motherwell.

FACT 80
1991 FIRST MANAGER NOT TO HAVE PLAYED FOR THE CLUB

In 1991 Liam Brady became only Celtic's eighth managerial appointment and the first who hadn't previously played for the club.

Billy McNeil was sacked in 1991 after two trophy-less seasons and for the first time the Board invited applications for the manager's job and interviewed candidates.

Although Brady had enjoyed a distinguished playing career with Arsenal, Juventus, Inter Milan and the Republic of Ireland, he had never played in Scotland and this was his first role as manager after retiring from playing the previous year.

The appointment of Brady had appeared a gamble and didn't come off. Although the side played attractive football he didn't win any trophies in his two full seasons in charge.

In 1990-91 Celtic finished third and only qualified for Europe after the civil war in Yugoslavia freed up an extra place for a Scottish team. However the subsequent UEFA Cup campaign ended in 2nd round humiliation as Celtic were thrashed 5-1 by Neuchatel Xamax in Switzerland, at the time their heaviest European defeat.

Brady's transfers were also disappointing, with big money being spent on Tony Cascarino, Gary Gillespie and Frank McAvennie only for them to fail to live up to expectations.

After a defeat at St Johnstone in October 1993 Brady's resignation was accepted by the board. He went on to manage Brighton & Hove Albion before returning to Arsenal in 1996 in a youth development role, where he remains today.

FACT 81

1992
OVERTURNING TWO GOAL EUROPEAN DEFICIT

During a difficult period for the club Celtic gave their supporters a night to remember on 30th September 1992 when they came from 2-0 down in the 1st leg to overcome Cologne in a UEFA Cup tie.

The lack of belief that Celtic could overturn the tie was reflected in the attendance of 30,747, way below what had seen previous great European nights. The last time the Celts had overturned a 2-0 first leg deficit was in 1968-69 against St Etienne and as Cologne began dangerously there looked little likelihood of it occurring on this occasion.

However two goals in the 36th and 39th minutes turned the tie on its head. First Paul McStay volleyed in from the edge of the area after a corner wasn't cleared properly and then Gerry Creaney turned in a John Collins drive to send Celtic's fans into raptures.

In the second half there was no sustained onslaught from Celtic, but nor did Cologne make any great effort to get an away goal that would surely have ended the tie.

With ten minutes remaining Collins received a Tom Boyd throw-in and beat two men before scoring with a low shot to complete a remarkable turnaround.

The joy of this win was short lived however as in the next round another German side, Borussia Dortmund, became the first side to beat Celtic in both legs of a European tie.

FACT **82**

1993
THE END OF THE STANDING JUNGLE

At the end of 1992-93 the Jungle, home to the most vociferous of Celtic's support, hosted standing spectators for the last time before its conversion to seating.

In the aftermath of the Hillsborough disaster, legislation was introduced outlawing terracing in all top flight grounds in Scotland and England, meaning that 5,000 seats would be installed on the Jungle.

The final home game of the season on 15th May 1993 was billed as the Jungle's Last Stand. All fans entering the terrace were given a certificate and there was parade of legends beforehand. Fans were invited to come in fancy dress, with the winner being a fan dressed as a parrot holding a sign that said 'Seats in the Jungle, I'm as sick as a parrot'.

Celtic beat Dundee 2-0, but that wasn't quite the end of the story, as a fortnight later Celtic Park was hosting the Scottish Cup final between Rangers and Aberdeen due to redevelopment at Hampden Park.

To avoid the untenable situation of Rangers fans being the last to stand on the Jungle, a match was arranged between Celtic's 1967 European Cup winning side and their 1968 equivalents from Manchester United. On 1st June 1993 over 20,000 turned out to give the famous old terrace one last send off.

FACT 83 — 1994 FOOTBALL'S MOST SUCCESSFUL SHARE ISSUE

In 1994 Fergus McCann completed his takeover of Celtic leading to the club generating more income from shares than any other in British football.

At the time Celtic was not in a healthy financial state, had not won a trophy since 1989 and was facing the difficult task of converting the terraced areas behind both goals into seating. In addition, relations between the board and fans were at an all time low.

McCann, a Celtic supporter in his youth who had emigrated to Canada and made his fortune from golfing holidays, gained control of the club and became its managing director. He then converted it into a public limited company, selling shares on the London Stock Exchange. Ex-director Michael Kelly, the subject of the fans frustration in the past, said buying lottery tickets was a better investment, but £14 million was raised from 10,000 investors, the largest flotation in British football history.

The shares issue stabilised the club and allowed for the re-building of Celtic Park into a 60,000 seat stadium, meaning that the club played at Hampden Park in 1994-95.

In addition to the stadium development, McCann also replaced manager Lou Macari with Tommy Burns and oversaw huge developments on the commercial side of the club. If it wasn't for his takeover the club wouldn't be where it is today.

FACT 84

1995 FIRST TROPHY IN SIX YEARS

A year after the Fergus McCann takeover, Celtic won their first trophy since 1989 to end their trophy drought.

Tommy Burns's first season in charge could have got off to a winning start much earlier but Celtic sensationally lost the League Cup final on penalties to 1st Division Raith Rovers.

In the Scottish Cup Celtic beat St Mirren, Meadowbank, Kilmarnock and Hibernian to reach the final where they faced another 1st Division side in Airdrie, determined not to be embarrassed again.

Pierre Van Hooijdonk got the Celts off to a perfect start when he headed them ahead in the ninth minute but the rest of the game was a fairly tedious affair. Celtic were wary of being to adventurous in case they were exposed at the back, while at the same time Airdrie didn't want to fall any further behind and kept it tight, meaning their attempts on goal were mainly from long range.

At the end of the game the celebrations were out of relief as much as joy, with Paul McStay continuing a tradition that saw every Celtic captain lift a trophy. With the club set to return to Celtic Park after a year playing home matches at Hampden, it also restored the optimism at the club that good times were ahead.

FACT 85

1997 CELTIC REFUTE WIMBLEDON LINK

In 1997 Fergus McCann was forced to pledge the club's allegiance to Scottish football after a report appeared stating that Celtic were looking to buy English side Wimbledon.

The growing status of the Old Firm amongst Europe's top clubs was indicated when Rangers were invited to take part in a six-a-side tournament in Amsterdam alongside Ajax, AC Milan and Liverpool. On 29th January the *Glasgow Evening Times* reported that Celtic were planning to buy Wimbledon, who were the English Premiership's worst supported club and had no ground of their own, in able to secure a place in the English top flight.

McCann was quick to dismiss the story, telling the *Celtic View* that all that had been discussed informally was the possibility of developing playing links outside Scotland but did stress this was within the framework of being part of a competitive Scottish league. He denied any suggestion that buying Wimbledon was on the agenda although did say there needed to be changes in Scottish football.

Although Wimbledon didn't need to be worried about any possible Celtic approach, five years later their fans did see their club taken from them when they were moved to Milton Keynes. A supporters owned club, AFC Wimbledon, was formed in 2002 and has managed to rise up the non-league pyramid into the English Football League.

FACT 86

1997 HENRIK LARSSON'S SHAKY START

At the beginning of 1997-98 Celtic's new Swedish striker had some moments to forget as he gave little indication of the great memories he would later bring for supporters.

Henrik Larsson was signed from Feyenoord that summer for £650,000. He was named as substitute for the opening game of the season at Hibernian but after coming off the bench with fifteen minutes remaining, he gave the ball away to Chic Charnley with his first touch. Charnley went on to score the winning goal in a 2-1 victory for Hibs who also hit the woodwork twice in the game.

The following week Larsson made some amends with the second goal in a 7-0 League Cup victory at Berwick Rangers, but in the second leg of a UEFA Cup 2nd Qualifying round tie against Tirol on 26th August, he scored an own goal on the stroke of half time. This left the score 2-2 on the night and with Celtic now trailing 4-3 on aggregate, they needed two more to progress.

Celtic did come back to beat Tirol 6-3 before going out on away goals to Liverpool in the next round. Larsson then overcame his early setbacks to score eighteen in all competitions from a deep role, making him the club's leading scorer as the league title was won.

The following season he became more of an out and out striker and scored 38 goals, earning him both the players' and writers' player of the year awards. Although a horrific leg break ruled him out for much of 1999-00 his prolific scoring continued on his return and by the time he left for Barcelona in 2004 he had scored 227 goals. He was named as the only non-Scottish player in the greatest ever Celtic team in 2002 and in 2006 was awarded the MBE for services to Scottish football.

FACT 87

1998 CELTIC STOP RANGERS TEN

In his one season as Celtic manager Wim Jansen won the Scottish League Championship to prevent Rangers overhauling the record of nine titles in a row.

At the start of the season Jansen, who had played against Celtic for Feyenoord in the 1970 European Cup final, was a surprise choice to replace Tommy Burns having spent the last three years managing in Japan.

Celtic got off to a disappointing start, losing their first two games but an eight match winning run lifted them into first place at the end of October. However there was then a setback with defeat in the first Old Firm game of the season and Celtic didn't return to the top of the table until the end of February.

Celtic had a great chance to open up a six point gap on Rangers on 12th April but they lost 2-0 at Ibrox and fell into second place on goal difference with four games left. The following Saturday Celtic beat Motherwell 4-1 and Rangers were beaten at Aberdeen the next day, but Celtic stuttered by drawing their next two games. The second of these at Dunfermline, which came a day after Rangers had lost 1-0 at home to Kilmarnock, meant the title went right down to the last day.

In front of 50,500 at a three quarter developed Celtic Park, a third minute goal from outside the area by Henrik Larsson calmed nerves but St Johnstone still had hopes of a European place so weren't rolling over. It wasn't until Harald Brattbakk scored with fifteen minutes left that the celebrations could really begin and at the end there were emotional scenes as fans sang 'You'll Never Walk Alone'.

The only disappointment was that Jansen resigned days afterwards, having found it increasingly difficult to work under Fergus McCann.

FACT **88**

2000
THE
YOUNGEST PLAYERS

In the second half of the 1999-00 season Celtic twice fielded the youngest ever players to wear the hoops.

In January 2000 manager John Barnes was sacked following a humiliating Scottish Cup defeat at home to 1st Division Inverness. Director of football Kenny Dalglish took charge until the end of the season and tried out a lot of new and younger players, with a total of twelve making their debuts between then and the end of the season.

On 5th April at home to Motherwell, a game which Celtic won 4-0, defender John Kennedy came on as a substitute with five minutes remaining. At 16 years and 231 days old this made him Celtic's youngest ever player, the previous record holder having been Roy Aitken at 16 years 290 days.

Then on 13th May midfielder Mark Fotheringham came on after an hour of the game in a 0-0 draw at St Johnstone. He was just 16 years 204 days old.

Despite these early starts, neither player enjoyed the same glorious career at Celtic as Aitken had. Fotheringham failed to live up to early promise, making only two more appearances before leaving for Dundee in 2003 and he has had a nomadic career since, playing in England, Switzerland, Germany and Cyprus.

Kennedy's story was one of frustration. After returning to the reserves, he became a regular in 2003-04 putting in some fine performances, only to suffer a cruciate ligament injury playing for Scotland which kept him out of the game for three years.

Although he returned to action in 2007-08, he was struck down again and missed the second half of the season.

In November 2009 he announced his retirement from playing after a re-occurrence during a loan spell at Norwich City.

FACT 89

2000 THE THREE AND A HALF MINUTE HAT-TRICK

When Celtic played Jeunesse Esch in the UEFA Cup on 24th August 2000 Mark Burchill created a European record for the fastest hat-trick.

The Celts were already 4-0 up from the first leg in Luxembourg and the opposition's cause wasn't helped when their star striker was not allowed to travel due to an invalid passport.

Despite the lead and the fact a number of regular players were rested, the game still attracted a crowd of 40,282, including eight intrepid Jeunesse fans who hadn't seen their side score away in Europe for thirteen years.

The game sparked into life between the twelfth and fifteenth minutes with Burchill's super fast hat-trick - the fastest scored in European club competition.

His first goal was a close range header, the second a neat shot past the keeper after controlling an Oliver Tebily pass and the third a tap in after being set up by Eyal Berkovic.

Stomach cramps forced Burchill to be substituted at half time, when the score was 4-0 after Berkovic had scored in the 22nd minute. After the break further goals from Berkovic, Vidar Riseth and Stilian Petrov completed a 7-0 rout.

Despite his hat-trick and Martin O'Neill's preference for him to stay and fight for his place, Burchill left for Birmingham on loan the following month and a year to the day after this hat-trick, was transferred to Portsmouth for £900,000.

FACT 90

2001
FIRST TREBLE SINCE JOCK STEIN DAYS

In 2000-01 Martin O'Neill completed a memorable first season in charge of Celtic when he led the club to a first treble since Jock Stein achieved it in 1969.

This was Celtic's first title since the Scottish Premier League was formed in 1998. It was never in doubt, with Celtic winning eleven of their first twelve games. This included a 6-2 thrashing of Rangers on 27th August, a game that saw Chris Sutton score the fastest goal in an Old Firm match after 51 seconds and Henrik Larsson find the net with an unbelievable chip. Dubbed the 'demolition derby', it was the highest derby score since the 7-1 1957 League Cup final and gave Celtic the belief that they were able to overhaul Rangers that season and go on to be dominant for the next few years.

Celtic lost only three games all season, two of them coming after the title had been secured with a 1-0 win over St Mirren when there were still five more matches remaining, one of them being at Ibrox where Rangers were beaten 3-0.

In the League Cup Celtic beat Raith Rovers, Hearts and Rangers to reach the final, where they beat Kilmarnock 3-0 thanks to a hat-trick from Henrik Larsson. The treble was completed on 26th May with a 3-0 win over

Hibernian in the Scottish Cup final. Jackie McNamara scored the first and the other two goals came from Larsson, taking his tally for the season to 53. At the end of the game the trophy was lifted jointly by Paul Lambert and club captain Tom Boyd, whose testimonial against Manchester United the following day was attended by over 57,000 fans.

FACT 91

2002 RECORD POINTS HAUL

In 2001-02 Celtic retained the Scottish Premier League title, the first time they had won back to back championships since 1981 and 1982, accumulating a record points haul in the process.

Celtic were never off the top of the table, winning seventeen out of the first eighteen games. Their one defeat was away to Aberdeen while Rangers were the only team to manage a draw at Celtic Park as Celtic won all but one of their home games.

The total record for the season as Played 38, Won 33, Drew 4, Lost 1, Goals for 94, Goals Against 19. The 103 points gained remains a Scottish league record and Rangers were a distant second on 85 points. Henrik Larsson was again a scoring sensation, hitting 29 goals from 33 games.

The title was clinched in the fifth from last game on 6th April with a 5-1 home win over Livingston, with Larsson scoring a first half hat-trick and John Hartson scoring the other two.

For the presentation of the trophy, Celtic's squad donned t-shirts bearing the slogan 'Hoops we did it again', with green and white balloons being let off and fans singing 'It's a Grand Old Team'.

Despite the league triumph there was disappointment in the cups, with Rangers beating Celtic in the Scottish Cup final and League Cup semi-final.

FACT 92

2003
80,000 FANS TRAVEL TO UEFA CUP FINAL

After re-asserting themselves domestically in the previous two years, Celtic imposed themselves on Europe again in 2002-03 by reaching the UEFA Cup final, leading to 80,000 fans travelling to southern Spain.

Initially Celtic's participation in the UEFA Cup was a disappointment as they had been knocked out of the Champions League qualifiers by Basle on away goals. In the 1st round they beat Lithuanians 10-1 on aggregate and after that the journey to Seville became magical as with each new round a harder task was faced yet still overcome.

Blackburn Rovers, Stuttgart and Celta Vigo were overcome on the way to the quarter final where Celtic faced Liverpool, winners of the competition in 2001. The chance to progress looked to have been lost after a 1-1 draw at Celtic Park but then the Celts refused to be intimidated in the second leg and won 2-0, John Hartson's 82nd minute goal causing delirium amongst the 3,000 away fans who knew there was now no way back for the Reds.

In the semi-final against Boavista, Celtic again drew the home leg 1-1 before winning 1-0 in Portugal thanks to a Henrik Larsson goal ten minutes from the end.

For the final against Porto in Seville, 80,000 Celtic fans are estimated to have travelled, arguably the greatest migration of football fans in history. Despite the much shorter distance they had to travel, Porto's fans were outnumbered three to one in the 70,000 capacity stadium.

Sadly Celtic couldn't bring the trophy home as Jose Mourinho's side, who won the Champions League a year later, beat Celtic 3-2 in extra time. Not one Celtic fan was arrested in Seville and this was acknowledged by the presentation of a FIFA Fair Play Award.

FACT **93**

2004
FIRST WIN OVER BARCELONA

In 2012-13 Celtic had a famous win over Barcelona in the Champions League but it wasn't the first time this had happened. Nine seasons earlier Celtic had also caused an upset against them in the UEFA Cup.

After finishing third in their Champions League group in 2003-04 Celtic dropped into the UEFA Cup and beat Czech side Teplice before being paired with the Catalan giants who were on an eight match winning run.

In the first leg at Celtic Park Celtic fended off some intense Barcelona pressure early on before creating some chances for themselves, but the game remained goalless at half time. Then there was a melee in the tunnel that led to Celtic keeper Rab Douglas and Barcelona's Thiago Motta being sent off.

In the 49th minute Javier Saviola was sent off for kicking and on the hour Alan Thompson gave Celtic the lead with a half volley from the edge of the six yard box. Douglas's replacement David Marshall was immense in goal as Barcelona sought an equaliser and he even saved a penalty from Ronaldinho. The following day Barcelona sports paper *El Mundo Deportivo* was glowing in its praise of the Celtic support, calling them the best fans on the continent.

Despite the 1-0 win there was still the second leg to overcome in the Nou Camp and in front of 8,000 travelling fans Celtic did a backs to the wall job to grind out a 0-0 draw. Marshall was again outstanding while young John Kennedy, in for the injured Bobo Balde, put in a solid defensive performance.

The defeat of Barcelona had showed that the previous season's run to Seville was no fluke, but Celtic were unable to make any further progress as they were beaten by Villareal in the quarter finals.

FACT 94

2004
25 MATCH WINNING RUN

When Celtic won the Scottish Premier League title in 2003-04 they again did so in sensational style, creating a record of winning 25 successive matches.

In 2002-03 Celtic had lost out on the title to Rangers by just one and after drawing their first game of the new season 0-0 at Dunfermline, they went on the run of wins that saw them score five or more goals on nine occasions and included two victories over Rangers.

The winning sequence began on 16th August 2003 with a 5-0 home win over Dundee United and the last in the run was on 29th February 2004 when Livingston were beaten 5-1 at Celtic Park.

When it finally came to an end with a 1-1 home draw with Motherwell on 14th March, it was just three days after the exhausting 1-0 UEFA Cup victory over Barcelona. Celtic didn't slip up after the second leg tough, winning 2-1 against Rangers at Ibrox to extend their lead at the top to nineteen points with eight games remaining.

On 19th April 2004, a 1-0 victory at Kilmarnock was sufficient to secure the title with six games remaining. It was a sweet moment for the club as the previous season a 4-0 victory at the same ground had not been enough to win the league, as Rangers had won 6-1 against Dunfermline.

Despite clinching the title Celtic were unable to complete the season unbeaten, losing their next two home games against Aberdeen and Dunfermline 2-1, the second of which came on the day that the trophy had was presented.

FACT 95

2006
REACHING THE CHAMPIONS LEAGUE KNOCKOUT STAGE

In 2006-07 Celtic progressed past the group stages of the Champions League for the first time, securing qualification with a memorable victory over Manchester United.

The group was so tight with four games played that Celtic knew they could still end up in either in first or last place. United, who were used to cruising through the group stages, had surprisingly lost their last game in Copenhagen and Sir Alex Ferguson was taking no chance with his line-up, fielding a first choice eleven for this game.

United played a patient game early on to quell the crowd and there were few early opportunities. Wayne Rooney's volley from outside the area on the half hour was the first time either keeper needed to be concerned. Jiri Jarosik and Shaun Maloney came on at half time but neither could liven up the Celtic attack, with Edwin Van Der Sar easily gathering any shots on his goal. United didn't threaten much with Wayne Rooney being extremely subdued and Christiano Ronaldo having a good run but firing his effort wide.

With ten minutes remaining Shunsuke Nakamura sent the crowd wild, scoring from a stunning thirty yard free kick after Jarosik had been fouled. United began to liven up, but Louis Saha hesitated when through on goal wrongly thinking he was offside, allowing Artur Boruc to save. United were then awarded a last minute penalty when Maloney handballed but Boruc saved Saha's kick.

The victory put Celtic top of the group and with the two teams below them -United and Benfica - playing each other in their last game they couldn't be overhauled. In the first knockout stage they put up a brave performance against eventual winners AC Milan, going out to an extra time goal in the San Siro.

FACT 96

2008 THREE SUCCESSIVE TITLES

In 2007-08 Celtic claimed a third successive Scottish Premier League title, making Gordon Strachan the first Celts manager to win a hat-trick of titles since Jock Stein during the nine in a row sequence.

Strachan had taken over as manager in 2005 after Martin O'Neill left to look after his seriously ill wife. His first two titles were won quite comfortably, but with seven games of 2007-08 to go Rangers looked certain champions, holding a seven point lead over Celtic with a game in hand.

However two of Celtic's remaining games were at home to Rangers and they won 2-1 and 3-2 within an eleven day period to give them some hope. These wins put Celtic five points ahead although Rangers still had three games in hand, their fixture backlog having built up by reaching the UEFA and Scottish Cup finals.

As Celtic beat Motherwell and Hibernian in their last two games Rangers slipped up by drawing two of their games in hand, ironically against the same two sides Celtic had beaten. This meant that on the last day of the season both teams were level on points with Celtic having a four goal lead.

Celtic beat Dundee United 1-0 thanks to a 72nd minute goal from Jan Vennegoor of Hesselink as Rangers lost 2-0 to Aberdeen to secure the title. It completed a great comeback for the Celts and the presentation of the trophy came at the end of an emotional week, the players wearing t-shirts in memory of former player and manager Tommy Burns whose funeral had taken place two days earlier after he had died of skin cancer.

FACT 97

2009 OVERCOMING HOME EUROPEAN DEFICIT

In a Champions League qualifying tie on 5th August 2009 Celtic beat Dynamo Moscow in Russia to progress for the first time in European competition after losing the first leg at home.

A week earlier Dynamo had won 1-0 at Celtic Park, thanks in part to some poor finishing. This was not the best start for new manager Tony Mowbray in his first competitive game in charge, having been appointed following Gordon Strachan's move to Middlesbrough. However things would take a turn for the better the next week.

At the Arena Khimki Dynamo didn't come out of their own half much in the first half, being happy to soak up the pressure and Celtic found it difficult to break their defence down. Two minutes before half time however Andrea Hinkel crossed and Scott McDonald headed home from close range to level the tie and give hope to the 200 Celtic fans that had travelled.

Dynamo came at Celtic early in the second half but a powerful shot went just wide and Hinkel cleared a header off the line. Celtic remained patient and didn't leave themselves exposed, then in injury time substitute Georgios Samaras beat two defenders before hitting a low shot past the keeper from the penalty spot.

Although Celtic had achieved a first, they were unable to carry the momentum into the next round against Arsenal, who won 5-1 on aggregate to progress to the group stages.

FACT 98

2010
AIDEN MCGEADY IS BIGGEST EXPORT

Early in the 2010-11 season Aiden McGeady was sold to Spartak Moscow for £9.5 million, making him Scottish football's most expensive export.

Signed as an eighteen year old in April 2004, McGeady scored on his debut against Hearts that month. He was able to play as an attacking midfielder or winger and voted young player of the year in his first three full seasons at the club.

However he also attracted criticism from some fans who felt his final delivery was poor and became a target for boo boys at other clubs due to his decision to opt for the Republic of Ireland at international level having been born and raised in Glasgow to Irish parents.

In 2007-08 though McGeady really got going, scoring eight goals from 39 starts and also weighing in with sixteen assists, receiving the accolade of Scottish players' player of the year. The following two seasons weren't as productive and he also had a much publicised falling out with Gordon Strachan. However in 2009-10 he was still voted Celtic players' player of the year.

When Russian side Spartak Moscow bid £9.5 million for him at the beginning of August 2010, it was too good an offer for the club to turn down given no Scottish club had ever received such a high transfer fee.

FACT 99

2011
21-1 AGGREGATE AGAINST ABERDEEN

During 2010-11 Celtic played Aberdeen on five occasions, winning every game and scoring 21 goals in the process.

The first encounter was in the league on 6th November when Celtic thrashed the Dons 9-0, a Scottish Premier League record and Aberdeen's biggest ever defeat. In the next league meeting at Celtic Park on 23rd January Celtic won again, but this time the scoreline was just 1-0.

On 1st February Celtic beat Aberdeen 3-0 at Pittodrie, a match that came just four days after the sides had met at Hampden Park in the semi-final of the League Cup, a game Celtic won 4-1.

There would be no more league games between the two teams due to Aberdeen being in the bottom six when the split took place, but the sides were drawn together again in the semi-finals of the Scottish Cup.

At Hampden Park on 17th April Andrew Considine was sent off in the first half but Anthony Stokes then had the subsequent penalty saved and it remained 0-0 at half time. But four minutes after the break Charlie Mulgrew's forty yard free kick went in and from then on the result was never in doubt as Celtic cruised to a 4-0 victory.

It added up to a total of 21 goals being scored against Aberdeen that season with just one conceded. Other teams weren't so generous however and Celtic ended up finishing second in the league and also lost to Rangers in the League Cup final, but did beat Motherwell 3-0 on 15th May to win the Scottish Cup.

FACT 100

2012 FOUR CAPTAINS AS THE LEAGUE IS WON

When Celtic won 6-0 at Kilmarnock on 7th April 2012 to secure the Scottish Premier League title, the captain's armband changed hands four times during the game.

A seventeen game winning run between November and February had seen Celtic pull clear in the title race and they found themselves even further ahead on 14th February when Rangers were deducted ten points for entering administration.

When they travelled to Rugby Park they were eighteen points clear with six games remaining and needed just a draw to be confirmed as champions.

Celtic were 4-0 up at half time and the fifth and sixth goals came in the last three minutes. The second half was unusual for the series of substitutions that saw the captain's armband pass from Scott Brown to Georgios Samaras to Charlie Mulgrew to Joe Ledley.

With Celtic's next game being in the Scottish Cup and the next home game being against Rangers, the championship trophy wasn't presented until four weeks later after a game with St Johnstone.

Although the league was won easily there was cup disappointment as Hearts knocked Celtic out of the Scottish Cup in the semi-final and in the final of the League Cup, Celtic were surprisingly beaten 1-0 by Kilmarnock, three weeks after the 6-0 game.

The most significant event came at the end of the season though when Rangers were wound up and clubs voted for the newco club to begin life in the 3rd Division, meaning it will be at least 2015-16 before the Old Firm are challenging each other for the league title again.

Sources

Athletic News
Celtic View
Glasgow Herald
Glasgow Evening Times
Scottish Umpire
www.scottish-football-historical-archive.com
www.statto.com
www.Thecelticwiki.com

The 100 Facts Series

Arsenal	978-1-908724-09-0
Celtic, *Steve Horton*	978-1-908724-10-6
Chelsea, *Kristian Downer*	978-1-908724-11-3
Everton	978-1-908724-12-0
Liverpool, *Steve Horton*	978-1-908724-13-7
Manchester City, *Steve Horton*	978-1-908724-14-4
Manchester United, *Iain McCartney*	978-1-908724-15-1
Newcastle United, *Steve Horton*	978-1-908724-16-8
Rangers	978-1-908724-17-5
Tottenham Hostpur	978-1-908724-18-2

ABOUT CHILDLINE

You can contact ***ChildLine*** about anything - no problem is too big or too small. If you're feeling worried, scared, stressed or just want to talk to someone you can contact ***ChildLine***. We're here to offer information and support whenever you need us.

We understand that it can be difficult to trust someone and tell them about what is happening or how you are feeling.

We want to help you feel confident when you use ***ChildLine*** and show what you can expect from us.

How can I contact ***ChildLine***?

Call free on 0800 1111 or visit http://www.childline.org.uk/

ChildLine Rocks is an annual charity rock concert organised under the auspices of ***ChildLine 20***, an independent committee set up to raise £2,000,000 for ***ChildLine*** to celebrate 20 years of ***ChildLine's*** existence.

Lightning Source UK Ltd.
Milton Keynes UK
UKOW06f1658090315

247559UK00002B/5/P